BULLETPROOF
YOUR JOB

ALSO BY STEPHEN VISCUSI

Nonfiction

On the Job:
How to Make It in the Real World of Work

BULLETPROOF YOUR JOB

4 SIMPLE STRATEGIES

TO RIDE OUT THE ROUGH TIMES
AND COME OUT ON TOP AT WORK

STEPHEN VISCUSI

COLLINS BUSINESS
An Imprint of HarperCollinsPublishers

A Karen Watts Book

HarperCollins books may be purchased for educational, business, or sales promotional use. For information, please write: Special Markets Department, HarperCollins Publishers, 10 East 53rd Street, New York, NY 10022.

FIRST EDITION

Designed by Jaime Putorti

Library of Congress Cataloging-in-Publication Data is available upon request.

ISBN–13: 978–0–06–1713606

08 09 10 11 12 DIX/RRD 10 9 8 7 6 5 4 3 2 1

My family and I have many friends who serve in the armed forces and they represent a rainbow of race, religion, and sexual orientation. I dedicate this book to all the men and women who serve our country throughout the world. In particular, this book is for those who serve in Afghanistan and Iraq, many of whom are returning home without a job to bulletproof.

I ask that we all help find them jobs upon their safe return. And I pray for those who will not returned because their first job—protecting our freedom—cost them their lives.

CONTENTS

INTRODUCTION

During tough economic times, the most important asset you have isn't your house or your savings. It's your job.

Like a lot of businesspeople, I have been influenced by Sun Tzu's classic *The Art of War*. I keep it on my desk at all times as a reminder that business is war, a sometimes brutal competition to succeed that you take seriously or not at all. Similarly, what goes on in the workplace is just one long season of *The Apprentice*, where each employee competes with the other to keep his job. Nasty stuff, eh? Well, work isn't a democracy. We don't get to vote for the way things should be, and nothing's very fair about how work works, either.

You're all pumped up with qualifications and experience? Great. Got a swanky Ivy League degree? How nice. Here's the cold hard truth: If you don't click with your boss, all that merit and pedigree won't get you anywhere when your job is on the line. People make this mistake all the time, thinking it's their good work and fine resume that matters. What really matters is what your boss thinks about you. That's it, in a nutshell. So ask yourself this simple question: Does my boss like me? If your answer is "No" or "I don't know," you're in trouble. Sounds unfair, but that's the way it is.

As a workplace and careers specialist and executive head-hunter, I've observed a familiar pattern when it comes to people and their jobs. When the economy is robust, people spend an inordinate amount of time scheming to get a better job or wondering whether they should change careers or rethink entirely what they're doing with their lives. It's the luxury of plenty—you have a secure job, so you're free to indulge in change and transformation.

When the economy is stressed or a particular industry is in crisis, however, I am asked over and over again, "How can I protect my job?" Gone are the daydreamy questions about the colors of parachutes. In their place are questions about job cutbacks and layoffs, and the need to feel secure is paramount. My answer to this question is always simple: If you really care about your job and career, you can start protecting it *right now.* If all you care about is your paycheck, there's almost nothing that will protect you from eventually being deselected in favor of another employee who's truly committed to his job. That's survival of the fittest at work in the workplace.

You must understand that your job is your most valuable asset, and your primary objective is to protect it.

So if your only worry is how to pay your rent, trying a few of the tactics in this book in order to stave off a pink slip might help you dodge a bullet today—maybe even tomorrow—but a casual observance isn't going to save your job in the long-term. That's because you can't fake bulletproofing your job. It requires a genuine commitment to a strategy to secure your job and career for the short *and* the long term. In for a penny, in for a pound.

Bulletproofing your job requires that you quit crying about merit and fairness and start improving your chemistry with your boss. Work is war, and if someone is going to get fired, let it be the guy your boss doesn't like, not you. If you don't have the stomach for this approach, hand this book to someone who does and watch *him* keep his job.

My no-nonsense strategy for bulletproofing your job is built on four simple precepts that will maximize your value and prospects for today *and* tomorrow:

Be visible. Be easy. Be useful. Be ready.

That's it. Easy to understand and supported by fifty straightforward, action-oriented tactics based on the way work *really* works that can help you start bulletproofing your job *right now*. The caveat is that you can't choose just one or two areas to work on and ignore the others. Being visible won't help you if you're not also being easy. And being useful won't do you any good if you're not ready for what might come next. They work only in tandem. But they do work.

Each of the fifty tactics in this book is meant to raise your consciousness and change your behavior. You don't do them once and check them off your list; you learn them and practice them and make them permanent habits. Some are easier than others to incorporate into your life; some can take a while to master. But together, they set you on a path of self-improvement, confidence, and security, the best place to be if you want to keep the job you have—and, when the time is right, to get the job you want.

Stephen Viscusi
stephen@viscusi.com
www.bulletproofyourjob.com

BULLETPROOF
YOUR JOB

1

BE VISIBLE

Here's the bulletproof truth: If your superiors don't see you or know who you are, you're very easy to let go. Out of sight, out of mind, and—poof!—you're gone. Accentuating and improving your physical presence and raising your overall profile at work are, together, the first steps toward locking down your job security.

I'll be honest: much of what you need to do is to create a *perception* that makes you more visible, more notable, and ultimately more valuable to your company. That means, for example, that you don't actually have to pull all-nighters twice a week to show how committed you are to your job. You do need to arrive at work before your boss and leave after she does in order to create the impression that you're there all the time. And you need to go out of your way to meet and engage people—coworkers, managers, even the CEO—who will unwittingly become a part of a team of people who will help you bulletproof your job.

I'm not being cynical, I'm being practical. And I'm not telling you to fake it, I'm telling you to make damn sure you're not invisible at the critical times when decisions are being made about who stays and who goes. **Because the invisible guy is the first to go.**

1. ARRIVE EARLY AND STAY LATE

The joke goes that 80 percent of success is just showing up. I disagree. I think that 80 percent of success is showing up *early*. More to the bulletproof point, it's showing up *earlier than your boss.* The rest is a magical combination of talent, exceptional effort, and good luck. For now, though, let's just concentrate on showing up early for work, shall we?

Arriving at work early shows your commitment and industriousness. Of course, you need to get there only five minutes before your boss or coworkers every day to come off as the world's most committed employee. Besides making it clear to your superiors that you take your job seriously enough to be more than on time, showing up early—before the phone starts ringing or your coworkers start bugging you—gives you valuable time to prepare for your day. Or rather, it gives you time to *look* as if you're prepared for your day. Sure, it's a bluff, but if you make it a habit, you'll always be ten steps ahead of the idiots who straggle in late all the time.

The same goes for meetings or conference calls or any other appointments. Be there early to get your ducks in a row. Showing up late, looking unprepared or discombobulated, isn't quite the impression to cultivate if you want to keep your job. Bosses and coworkers hate when you show up late for meetings. *Hate* it. So don't.

JUST SO YOU KNOW

It doesn't matter if your company pays for your health club membership or even provides an on-site health facility—that's to make *it* look good, not to help you lower your cholesterol. Installing a swanky gym on the premises is strictly for PR purposes; it looks great when the company is being profiled on *60 Minutes*, but no one expects you to actually use it. Same goes for those nifty pool tables, nap rooms, and massage services offered by youthful and progressive CEOs. If the stock in your publicly traded company is in free fall, I guarantee the pool-playing slackers will be sent packing long before the CEO's private jet is listed on eBay. So admire those perks, brag about them to your friends, but, whatever you do, don't get caught using them.

No one likes a martyr, but managers *love* an employee who is willing to stay late in order to get the job done. Be willing to do whatever is necessary timewise in order to complete a project. This doesn't have to make you a slave to your job or a doormat for your boss; do it on an as-necessary basis, and it will demonstrate your commitment to your work.

Here's another easy bluff: Don't stay late, just stay later. Leaving a mere ten minutes after your boss has gone reinforces the impression that you're the world's most committed employee. It also shows that you're not a clock-watching nine-to-fiver. People who say "I'm outta here" the minute the whistle blows every day are bound to be "outta there" come downsizing time.

While you're at it, skip the two-hour lunches—you don't want to be MIA when something important is going down at the office. And you don't want to give the impression that what you do on your lunch hour—such as shopping, going to the gym, or

JUST SO YOU KNOW

Working through lunch to meet a pressing deadline is one thing. Eating at your desk every day is another. As a general rule, don't do it. Here's why:

► It's inappropriate. Your desk is your workstation, not the dinner table. You wouldn't (or would you?) use a fingernail clipper at your desk, neither should you use a knife and fork there. The separation of work and personal activities—including eating—is just good manners on the job.

► It's inconsiderate to your coworkers. No one should have to smell your tuna sandwich or watch you picking popcorn out of your teeth at your desk.

► It doesn't look professional. Even if you brown-bag it every day, eat in the office dining area or off site.

visiting the dentist—is more important than the work that's waiting for you on your desk. Appointments are for weekends, and working out is for before or after work. If you must take care of personal affairs during your lunch hour, be clandestine about it. No one needs to know you're at your techno-Pilates class or getting your eyebrows waxed—especially your boss.

Do step out of the office for lunch or even just a short walk to clear your head. Better yet, do it while your boss is at lunch, so she never sees you not working and never has to wonder where you are. But keep it to twenty minutes or less, unless you're having a business lunch, in which case make sure your boss knows where you are, and aim to keep it to an hour, ninety minutes tops.

There's always someone in the office who can't sit still, always getting up for a cup of coffee, visiting the bathroom ten times a day, endlessly making the rounds to chat with friends. This is not a supereffective visibility strategy. Avoid frequent breaks—you don't want your boss thinking you're away from your desk more than you're behind it. And when it comes to the nearly extinct cigarette break, I say go ahead and smoke like a chimney in your private life, but don't let your superiors see you loitering in front of the building dragging on a cigarette. *Everything* is wrong with that image.

Be judicious in taking time off. That monthlong bike tour of Italy? Take it another time. No one's saying you shouldn't take a vacation or long weekend to which you are entitled. You should just be very aware of timing and the impression your taking time off gives to your boss and colleagues, especially when things are tough at work. Weekend weddings are generally acceptable; long holidays—especially when business is either busy or slumping— are not. This isn't France, you know!

Pay close attention to exactly what's going in the office when you make plans. Think about spacing out your vacation time in chunks of three or four days at a time instead of two weeks at once, so you're not out of the picture for too long a stretch.

JUST SO YOU KNOW

Smoking is a bad habit, unattractive, and harmful to your health. So don't do it—unless your boss does. Smokers love other smokers, and bosses who smoke love employees who share the habit. What better time to bond with your boss than leaning against the front of your building puffing away? A sneaky guy I used to know actually took up smoking when he re- alized that his boss was a nic addict. Not good for his lungs but he enjoyed a connection with his boss that his coworkers didn't.

Same goes for sick days. If you have a hacking cough or a 104° fever, by all means, keep all those germs at home where they belong. But if you're just hung over from watching the NCAA basketball finals until 1:00 A.M. with your buddies, suck it up and get to work. You don't want to be known as the guy who's always out sick.

And by the way, you *really* don't want to be known as someone who needs "mental health days." Britney Spears needs mental health days—lots of them. *You* need to bulletproof your job. So if you don't have a blazing fever, you better be at your desk at work.

Finally, even if your job allows for you to work from home instead of at the office—even just the occasional one day a week— think hard before doing that, especially when turbulence is in the air. Because soon enough you'll be "working from home" plenty; home workers are always the first to get fired. Your boss or your clients won't remember why you're valuable if you're *not there*.

▶ ▶ ▶ **Be punctual.**
▶ ▶ ▶ **Create the perception that you're always there.**

2. LOOK GOOD

Even if you work in a Monday-through-Friday casual dress environment, the way you dress should send a message that you're serious about your job. Or, more to the point, that you're serious about *keeping* your job. So go to your closet right now and map out a strategy to dress as if you mean it.

First of all, consider your company's dress code. If it's not

SHOES MAKE THE MAN . . . AND THE WOMAN

Shoes are near the top of the list of things people notice first about a person. To be sure you're sending the right shoe message every day at work, women should not wear sneakers; glittery, fussy, or open-toed shoes; or crazy-high heels. Men should wear black or brown shoes (not boots) that are well made and not trendy. Wear the best-quality shoes you can afford; go into hock if you have to so you wear shoes that make the most emphatic "success" statement possible. In the case of shoes, price happens to be a decent indicator of quality, so do a little research and cross-referencing between, say, Nordstrom, Brooks Brothers, and Barney's to figure out your high-water mark of affordability. Keep them shined and in good repair; worn heels and scuffed toes on even the finest shoes will peg you as a down-and-outer, not an up-and-comer.

spelled out in the employee manual, take a look around to make an assessment. What do the top-level managers wear every day? The midlevel managers? How about your supervisor? Your colleagues? If you're not dressing better than your colleagues and at least as well as your supervisor, you're missing an easy opportunity to make a subtle but positive impression on the powers that be.

Take your cue from the folks who run the show. If the CEO wears a power suit and tie every day, you should wear something just as serious and purposeful that's appropriate for your job. But even if all the top managers wear Hawaiian shirts, you still need to aim high yourself. The idea is to wear what suits you but in the general genre of your boss; it's the kind of subtle flattery that will get you everywhere.

None of this means you should go from jeans and Birkenstocks to an Armani suit overnight; if you suddenly start dressing up, your colleagues will think you're interviewing for a new job. Which is no way to keep the job you have, right? So instead of dressing up, start dressing upward. Look for ways to sharpen your appearance without looking as if you've gone and had a total makeover.

Start by taking a good hard look at your clothes. Try on every item of clothing you regularly wear to work in front of a mirror. Then set aside anything to which you answer "no" to any of the questions below:

- ▶ Is it well made, clean, and in good repair?
- ▶ Does it fit me well?
- ▶ Does it make me look professional?
- ▶ Does it make me look successful?
- ▶ Would I wear it to an important meeting?

Even if this exercise forces you to retire half of your usual wardrobe from work duty, you don't have to go out and buy new threads. With a little common sense, the remaining clothes you have will do just fine. Wearing one excellent suit three times a week is infinitely better than wearing five different outfits that don't market you as a capable, confident, can-do employee.

While you're doing the mirror test, take a look at your hair. Smartly styled hair is the new power suit, easily as important as what you're wearing. And worth every penny you spend getting it right. So:

- ▶ Do you keep up a good haircut, or are you usually overgrown?
- ▶ Is the hairstyle you wear appropriate to your age?

► Is the color flattering?

► Is the color current? (Meaning, are your roots showing or do you have unintended stray gray hairs?)

If the answers to these questions are "no" or "I don't know" get yourself to the best hairstylist you can afford *right now* to sort out your hair situation. Don't skimp on hairstyle or color. I don't mean you should get a $600 Sally Hershberger haircut if you're making $600 a week. But don't end up with a bargain style at Supercuts that you'll sorely regret, either. Just budget for a good

TOP WORK WARDROBE MISTAKES

► Revealing clothing (cleavage, visible belly, rose tattoo above your butt crack)

► Poorly fitting clothing (muscleman tight, too tight anywhere, or too loose everywhere)

► Age-inappropriate clothing (for example, a pleated schoolgirl mini on anyone but a schoolgirl)

► Any clothing with logos on it

► Inappropriate shoes (slutty footwear and mandals, for example)

► Too much makeup (including Dracula lip liner and freaky fake fingernails)

► Too much perfume or cologne (frankly *any* perfume or cologne is too much)

N.B. If you have to ask yourself whether you're making any of these mistakes, you are.

TRUE STORY

Anna was a junior-level account rep at a hip dot-com agency. Like her co-workers, she enjoyed the low-key feel of her workplace, including casual attire, flexible hours, and a generally collegial, creative atmosphere. She was easy to recognize by the elaborate dreadlocks she'd worn since college, as well as for the dragon tattoo that curled around her entire right arm and the nose ring dangling from her left nostril. She was happy doing a job she enjoyed in a place where her personal expression was embraced.

All that ended the day her company learned its VC funding had fallen through and Anna was included in the first round of layoffs. Why her? While her colleagues appreciated her unique personal style, her boss had to make a choice between Anna and a more conservative coworker who was more presentable when pitching to much-needed potential clients.

haircut—regularly, and at least two weeks before an important event—because it's *that* important.

Now follow these basic rules for a bulletproof look:

▶ Dress to be noted, not noticed. Whether your style is classic and conservative or more contemporary, looking good always comes down to wearing clothing that flatters you and suits your body. Dressing appropriately for your job and your personality lets you be who you are but always look professional. That said, fads and fashion statements (ahem, that would be you, young lady, the one thinking about wearing high-waisted hot pants and knee-high gladiator sandals to work!) do not belong in the work-place. Neither do obnoxiously loud colors, jangly jewelry, or dangerous or ill-fitting footwear. All that's a little too much you, okay?

▶ Use accessories to dress upward. A good watch, a silk scarf or necktie, smart eyeglasses—all send signals of quality and self-assuredness. So do an expensive haircut and neatly manicured hands (this goes for both men and women). And finally, I have three words for you: Crest White Strips. A bright white smile is the best, most bulletproof accessory of all.

▶ Give extra care to your daily grooming. When you show up at the office with wet hair or needing a shave, you're saying that you don't care enough to pull yourself together for work. Clean hair and fingernails and brushed teeth—that's stuff your mother taught you. Well-tended facial hair (including eyebrows, nose, and ear hair), fresh breath, neutral body odor—that's the stuff you ought to pay attention to but might overlook. These are the details that send silent positive messages about you to everyone around you. Or negative messages that can put your job in peril. You choose.

▶ P.S. Regarding facial hair, an extremely tidy beard or mustache may be appropriate in a workplace where they are clearly accepted. After you take a good look around, though, don't be surprised to discover they're not. In any case, follow the boss's lead. Regarding the "styling" of eyebrows, men *and* women: do

JUST SO YOU KNOW

One of the best ways I know to initiate, reinforce, or improve the chemistry between you and your boss is to think of yourself as his Mini Me. Follow his or her lead in wardrobe, general demeanor, and communication style. Being a bit of a Mini Me is subtly flattering to your boss, and it ensures that you're basically behaving in a way you already know he approves of. Plus, who's going to fire his Mini Me?

not overdo. And those intentional 9 A.M. five o'clock shadows? I think they give the impression that you never made it home last night, and they're a good idea only if you're a fashion photographer or a European architect—or if your boss has one.

▶▶▶ *Dress upward.*
▶▶▶ *Get an excellent haircut.*
▶▶▶ *Have a bright, white smile.*

3. PAY ATTENTION TO DETAIL

I don't care what anybody says, you *do* have to sweat the small stuff. Whether you're the front-desk receptionist or the CEO, your mastery of detail can be the difference between succeeding and failing on a simple clerical task or a multibillion-dollar deal. If there is one person in the workplace who *might* be considered indispensable, it's the person who is on top of the details.

That's easier said than done, though. Being detail-oriented is one of those qualities that's much admired and rarely possessed. It's like being good with languages or numbers; it comes either naturally or not at all. Fortunately, there are plenty of ways to improve your detail skills even if you're an oblivious boob.

▶ Be organized. This is the A-number-one most important thing you can do to help yourself pay attention to detail. Being organized helps you work with an ease and efficiency that never fail to make you look good. In particular, your workspace should be organized so that whatever you need is at your fingertips when you need it most. This means that everything has a place, you can access what you need without effort, and someone else could eas-

SPELLING COUNTS

Don't get me started on how spell-checkers are turning us into a nation of dunces. The fact is, no matter how well a program sweeps up after our atrocious spelling, it's not going to catch everything. If you can't spell or you use bad grammar, you might as well pack up your desk right now. It's the kind of inattention to detail that sets you apart from others—in the bad way. So reread your documents, letters, and e-mails before sharing. *Especially* your e-mails. Before you send an e-mail, be sure it's addressed to the correct person—Karen from accounting probably doesn't need to see your note to Karen, the dancer you met last night at the Kit Kit Club. Proofread your outgoing e-mail, too. Bad spelling—the kind that e-mail seems to make worse—can make even the smartest person look like a junior high school dropout. If you press "send" without proofing the contents and confirming the intended recipients, you may as well write "Fire me" in the subject line. If you must, find a colleague who's willing to proof your work for you.

Finally, as much as I think automated spell-check has set our collective intellect back about ten thousand years, install it on your BlackBerry or iPhone *right now.* Corresponding on the run doesn't tend to highlight your communication skills, especially when it's all botched up with missing words and bad spelling.

ily be directed by you to find something in your workspace in your absence. (Remember that vacation that was almost ruined by frantic calls from the office hunting for a contract lost in your "file pile," which was obscured by a half-eaten box of Mallomars?)

In a perfect world, being organized means no piles, no clutter, no obstacles. In a bulletproof world, however, piles are not a bad thing. They're a part of the fine art of looking busy. Better to be thought of as superbusy than anally organized, I always say. Just don't let important details fall through the cracks—or heaps—on your desk.

▶ Be thorough. This is what they call dotting the *i*s and crossing the *t*s. Seems as if you shouldn't have to tell someone to do that, as the *i*s and the *t*s aren't going to do you much good without those dots and the crosses, am I right? But you'd be surprised how many big problems are the result of sloppy mistakes. Double-check instructions, pay attention to deadlines, review your work before passing it on. Follow up to be sure it was received, that it was done right, and whether anything else is necessary. It is a tremendous compliment when someone refers to your work as thorough.

▶ Take notes. Keep a single notebook with you at all times to keep track of names, dates, phone conversations, or instructions you receive (no one likes to have to explain—again—how to change the toner in the copier). Other random but important details will end up in your notebook, and will you ever be a hero

JUST SO YOU KNOW

You might as well admit that when you claim you "lost all your work" it usually means you never did it in the first place and you're trying to buy time to get it done. Your boss can smell this a mile away, and while she might let you get away with it once, twice will try her patience, and three times will let her know you're a liar and you think she's stupid. So do your work and back it up. In the long run, it's easier than making up bigger and bigger dog-ate-my-homework whoppers that will eventually cost you your job, I promise.

when you're the only one who has them. Think moleskin rather than Hello Kitty—even your notebook sends a message.

▶ Keep a calendar. You'd be surprised how many people trust their reality TV-addled brains to remember important appointments. Whether you keep a paper datebook or a calendar on your computer or PDA, enter every single engagement (personal and professional) on the same calendar. Nothing looks more foolish than forgetting a meeting.

▶ Respond to e-mail and telephone messages quickly and efficiently. Don't be the person who takes a week to answer a simple e-mail or return a call. Be the one who manages detail-driven exchanges swiftly and effectively.

▶ Back yourself up. Losing an important document or your entire archive of e-mail because you weren't backed up is even more foolish than forgetting a meeting. If you're not automatically backed up by your company's system or you keep important work on your home computer, back your own files up. It's your responsibility to be sure your own work is secure.

Bulletproofing your job is more about being street smart and having good chemistry with your boss than it is about being organized. So don't think of all this as being Container Store organized; think of it as being-savvy-and-paying-attention-to-details-that-can-save-your-bacon organized.

▶▶▶ *Don't be a slob.*
▶▶▶ *Be thorough and efficient.*
▶▶▶ *Keep a notebook.*

4. LISTEN UP

The mighty motivational speaker Zig Ziglar once said that when you talk, you say something you already know, but when you listen, you learn something that someone else knows. That's listening in a nutshell: shutting up and really taking in what someone else is saying.

How is listening a way to be visible at work? For one thing, it's the opposite of not listening. Zoning out in meetings, losing track of what's going on during a conference call, making your grocery list in your head while you're having a conversation with someone—that's the kind of not listening that moves you to the top of the list of expendable personnel.

Active, genuine listening is best way to be sure you're in the know—and that the right people know that you're in the know. When listening:

▶ Give your undivided attention. Turn off your cell phone, put away your BlackBerry, get out your notebook, and

JUST SO YOU KNOW

Don't you hate it when people don't pay attention when you're talking to them? Here's why someone stops listening: He has a pathetic attention span. There are too many distractions, including that cell phone vibrating in his pocket. He probably thinks listening is a chore, not a tool. He doesn't really understand what you're saying. He's too busy thinking about his own opinions to listen to what you're saying. Or finally, there's a very good chance you're not giving him something interesting or useful to listen to. Oh, that smarts.

make eye contact with the speaker. Good eye contact is 50 percent of the successful chemistry you need to have with the people around you. In short, be present.

▶ Don't jump to conclusions. Just because you think you've gotten the gist of the speaker's message, it doesn't mean you can turn down the volume and start daydreaming about your trip to Vegas.

▶ Practice 360° listening. You listen in order to learn, so listen to everyone in the room. And be open to alternative points of view.

▶ Confirm what you've heard. This is especially important in one-on-one conversations. If you're not sure you understand what has been said, ask the speaker to confirm his meaning. "I just want to be sure I heard you correctly: Are you saying . . . ? " Or come right out and say, "Could you please repeat that? I'm not following you." This helps avoid misinterpretation all around.

▶ Don't interrupt. The fact that it's bad manners is a good enough reason not to interrupt. Ever. It's also one of the most annoying and self-destructive habits a person can have. Let a speaker complete his thought—while really listening to what he's saying—before offering your own.

▶▶▶ *Pay attention when people speak.*
▶▶▶ *Be sure of what you've heard.*
▶▶▶ *Don't interrupt.*

JUST SO YOU KNOW

You are your cell phone's ring tone. Which means don't have a ridiculous Looney Tunes ringtone, the cell phone equivalent of an e-mail address like foxymama@hotmail.com. That's tacky and silly. It also means turn your cell phone off at work. Period. Every time your cell phone rings when you're on the job, you're alerting your boss that you're not working.

5. SPEAK UP

Outgoing people and those with naturally strong communication skills are obviously more likely to pipe up in a group setting than others are.

The problem, for those of you who make up the quieter population, is that if you don't say anything, no one will know that you're smart or curious or creative or that you have a clever sense of humor, all qualities that can significantly distinguish you from your coworkers and give you a leg up when the company's chips are down. When people are losing jobs and you want to bulletproof yours, it's critical to be seen *and* heard. Action and words are of equal importance in showing you're alive at your job and want to keep it. So go out of your way to verbally assert yourself in all aspects of your work.

The easiest way to speak up is to start asking questions. It shows that you're willing to learn and that you're smart enough to know what you *don't* know. Ask for clarification early, and you won't find yourself barreling off in the wrong direction due to unanswered questions you were too afraid to ask. Your boss will be glad you asked, trust me. You'll also win fans among your col-

HOW TO SAY WHAT'S ON YOUR MIND

▶ Be confident. If you're so nervous that dry mouth and sweaty palms keep you from speaking up at work, practice in front of the mirror until you feel sure of yourself. Better yet, take one of those amazing Dale Carnegie courses that can turn just about anyone into a confident speaker. Every time you venture to speak, you'll feel more comfortable doing it again.

▶ Get to the point. When making a point or asking a question, don't blather on and on, using jargon or showing off what you know. Instead of coming off as smart, you'll come off as talky or, worse, as a self-important blowhard.

▶ Be diplomatic. Now's not the time to pick a fight with a coworker who disagrees with you or to correct your boss when he has misspoken. If you feel that you must correct someone's mistaken statement, do it tactfully and in private. And avoid critiquing others; *no one* likes to be critiqued, mostly because it's almost always negative. Just compliment them on their ideas and then offer your own.

▶ Show intelligence. Speaking up is your chance to show your smarts. But if you don't have anything insightful or intelligent to contribute, don't speak for the sake of speaking. That's almost always what makes meetings last longer than they should, and you know how much that gets on *your* nerves.

leagues for being willing to raise your hand, as they probably have the very same questions.

Offer suggestions. If someone running a meeting asks the group for ideas and you think you have a good one, say it out

ASK YOURSELF:

▶ Do I speak up regularly?

▶ Do I speak clearly?

▶ Do I share original thoughts?

▶ Do I help improve the dialogue?

▶ Do I improve the way I am perceived when I speak up?

loud. No one can read your mind, and you get no credit for an idea you haven't expressed. Not every suggestion you have will be a good one, and no one needs to know what you think about every single thing. But a carefully offered suggestion or opinion on the right subject at the right time can shine a positive light on you. If a higher-up offers you a chance to share your opinion and you have something intelligent to say, grab it. She'll admire you for taking the risk and for having a mind of your own. (Though she'll admire you more if you make it look as if it was *her* idea.) In the end, you want to be perceived as someone who is confident enough in his own intelligence and creativity to be an effective brainstormer.

▶▶▶ *Ask smart questions.*
▶▶▶ *Make thoughtful suggestions.*
▶▶▶ *Speak clearly.*

6. VOLUNTEER TO LEAD

Even if no one has ever mistaken you for General Patton, offering to take the lead shows you have a stomach for risk, the capacity to learn, and the desire for accomplishment that others might not possess. Search for opportunities to lead and to expand your leadership skills and experience. You'll increase your visibility *and* the trust your supervisor is willing to place in you to get the job done.

The trick to learning to take the lead is to start small. You're not gunning for a promotion or to be anyone's boss. You just want to get a chance to be in the driver's seat on an assignment and see how it feels. Volunteer to head a project that no one else

WHERE YOU LEAD

A good leader has the ability to motivate others to get a job done well and on time. And—to paraphrase Dwight Eisenhower a little—to get them to do it because *they* want to do it. Assuming everyone on your team is reasonably capable of doing the work required, it's the motivation you need to provide. Here are a few ideas for getting your people pumped up:

▶ Make them feel they're in capable hands. Have a plan, be prepared, and roll up your sleeves to work alongside them.

▶ Be sure all involved have a big picture of the project so they understand their role in the outcome. Show them that you believe everyone's individual contribution is important to the whole.

▶ Be upbeat and encouraging. Show enthusiasm and confidence even if things get a little dicey. Keep everyone focused on solutions instead of problems. Be generous with positive reinforcement.

TRUE STORY

Though some people say leaders are born, not made, I say anyone can learn to lead enough to make a noticeable difference. Take Terry, a junior advertising sales account executive at a television station in Houston. As a young African-American man in a competitive field, he believed he had to do a better job than his colleagues in order to distinguish himself. Seeing an opportunity, he called on his postcollege experience working on the fringes of Washington politics and offered to take on the sales of the station's political advertising. No one else was remotely qualified to take that leadership role for the station—including Terry when he first took it—but he saw a leadership vacuum and filled it, developing invaluable expertise and exposure along the way. Now he's a senior-level sales exec, handling high-profile commercial accounts as well as the political work for which he's become so valued by his employer.

wants. That way you're not competing with anyone for it and your boss is likely to be grateful that you offered at all.

Make a game plan for getting the job done. Figure out what you need to learn to make it happen. Then ask one or two others to play a supporting role. Being a one-man band is impressive, but not as impressive as motivating and guiding others to accomplish something together. Meet your deadline, overdeliver on quality, and give your colleagues credit for their help. Then volunteer for another project. And another.

Taking the lead on a project-by-project basis gives you a chance to cultivate new skills and expertise. You'll learn to plan, strategize, and execute better. You'll learn how to build a team. You'll improve your communication skills. You'll gain the trust of your colleagues and the confidence of the people in charge. Be the guy your boss can count on to say, "Put me in, Coach!" Because when people around you at work are dropping like flies, he'll know you're not afraid to take the lead.

So when there's a chance to run a meeting or to take a leadership role in planning or executing an event related to your work, take it. Volunteer to head a committee or lead a research or problem-solving initiative. Besides giving you career-boosting experience and broader knowledge, these opportunities will raise your profile with the higher-ups and increase the value of your contribution to the company.

▶▶▶ *Look for opportunities to show you can lead.*
▶▶▶ *Hone your leadership skills on a project-by-project basis.*

7. MAKE PRESENTATIONS

If making presentations isn't already part of your job, it should be. It's a great way to put your confidence, mastery of a subject,

JUST SO YOU KNOW

For some people, making public presentations will never *ever* be their thing. You can practice forever and still fail miserably every time. Maybe you're uncomfortable with how you look or you sweat too much or a stutter you had in second grade comes back like a bad rash. Whatever. The bottom line is that you should lead with your strengths when you're bulletproofing your job. So if presentations are just not happening for you, don't do them. The easiest way to make a target of yourself is to stand up in front of everyone and show how inept you are.

REALLY GOOD POWERPOINT PRESENTATIONS

PowerPoint is the best thing that ever happened to presentations. It's simple to use and, in the right hands, it can help make an emotional connection with your audience that sells them on your message. In the wrong hands, it can brutally amplify the pain of a poor presentation for everyone involved, including you.

The marketing guru Seth Godin preaches against the "really bad PowerPoint" he sees all the time in presentations. Of course, it's not the PowerPoint that's bad, it's the way the presenter uses it. Here are a few of Seth's simple rules for using PowerPoint for good instead of evil:

► Use cue cards, not the words on the screen, for your speaking notes. And limit the number of words you use on the screen to no more than six per slide.

► Use sharp slides and images with emotional impact that reinforce and illustrate your message, not repeat it. No one wants to have to read along with the words you're saying. Boring. In fact, it's twice as boring.

► Distribute a document that summarizes or further elaborates on your message. Do not distribute a printout of your PowerPoint presentation. And do not distribute the document until *after* your presentation. That way your audience will listen to you instead of skimming the document while they tune you out.

and communication skills on display. And if you don't already have those skills, it's the world's best way to develop them.

Start small. Look for opportunities to present the results of a project or a new concept to your most immediate work group. Use a low-key scenario like this to get comfortable speaking in

TRUE STORY

Kendall could write great pitches for her innovative ideas but was too shy to do her own oral presentations. So she'd enlist someone else in her department to lead the dog-and-pony show and got only a fraction of the credit she deserved for her work. Every time she let someone pinch-hit for her, she not only gave away her creative equity, she passed up a chance to be noticed, recognized, or even advanced. After two colleagues were promoted after presenting *her* ideas, Kendall got herself some public speaking training. And the next time she had a big idea, it was Kendall at the podium collecting her own kudos.

front of others and to create a presentation formula that suits you. Here's how to get your head in the presentation game:

▶ Always consider your audience. Believe it or not, every audience is rooting for you to succeed, which gives you a leg up from the get-go. But understand that everyone shows up expecting a benefit. Whatever the purpose of your presentation, send them away with something they can use.

▶ Have a very clear idea of what you're trying to accomplish. Are you presenting a report? Explaining a process? Gathering support or building consensus? Motivating? Training? Your presentation formula will be pretty much the same, but visualizing your desired result will help shape the content.

▶ Stick to concise points, accessible language, and appealing and useful anecdotes and visuals your audience can see (use large enough type) and will remember. Complicated charts and graphs? *Zzzzzzz.* A short but snazzy Power-Point presentation with photos of chimps (chimps *always* work) and unexpected captions? A hearty round of applause.

▶ Finally—and this is Public Speaking 101—make eye contact with your audience, speak at a moderate pace, and smile. Practice your presentation with a friend or trusted colleague. Double-check that your equipment works and that your visuals are in the correct order.

Besides creating a little neon light over your head that says, "Over here! Look at me!," giving presentations helps you learn to explain your thinking or results to your colleagues, solicit constructive feedback, and be an effective advocate for your own work. Those are long-term, lifetime bulletproof skills.

▶▶▶ **Present what you know in a clear, concise, appealing way.**

▶▶▶ **Practice presenting every chance you get.**

8. REPRESENT YOUR COMPANY

Attending conferences, seminars, or professional development meetings on behalf of your company is a uniquely effective way to raise your profile. By acting as the face of your company at a gathering of leaders and colleagues in your field, you get an instant shot of credibility and authority that you wouldn't have if you were back at your desk at work nibbling on a Pop-Tart. And you get that just for showing up! If you make a point of extracting every bit of value out of the experience, you'll go home with your pockets full of bulletproof schwag.

First, you generally get points just for volunteering to attend a conference. Unless they're featured speakers, higher-ups tend not to want to go themselves, preferring to send junior levels to represent the company and bring back conference booty. That booty isn't the cheesy commemorative tote bag and mouse pad, it's information about what's going on in your industry—including gossip and other gory details—and new skills and insights you can share with the team.

Conferences aren't always fun. Okay, *mostly* they're not fun. Unless a conference features a dazzling cast of speakers or cutting-edge seminars or workshops, you may have to look hard for the nugget of something new to take back to your colleagues. But that's what you're there for: to observe, collect, and represent. And to network like mad, of course.

That's why your number-one job when representing your company at a conference is to look sharp, act sharp, and make connections. Not the mindless business card-swapping kind, but the substantive kind that turns a new acquaintance into a lasting

TOP CONFERENCE MISTAKES

▶ Not having an effective pitch about your company

▶ Hanging out with people you already know

▶ Talking too much about yourself

▶ Peddling gossip rather than collecting it

▶ Not following up with people you meet

▶ Arriving late, leaving early, and skipping events

▶ Getting drunk, dirty dancing, sleeping with other conference attendees resource. That smart guy you talked to for an hour at the opening reception and sat next to again at the second-day workshop? He may be a potential client, a valuable reference, or even a future employer. But you'll never know that unless you make a good connection and follow up by staying in touch.

When you return from a conference, you should have at least one practical insight to share with your colleagues. You should have made at least one meaningful connection—someone you can fold into your network. And if your boss runs into someone who was also at that conference, that person should be able to say you made a great impression. So do it. Here's how:

▶ Dress upward. Now isn't the time to kick back and wear a baseball cap and flip-flops because you're at a weekend conference at a golf resort in Tampa. Whatever the dress code for the conference—which is usually indicated in the registration materials or strongly suggested by the location—dress a couple of degrees above. Because you're going to be in the company of people you don't know, go with khaki conservative rather than Club Med hot.

▶ Stay for the whole conference. Avoid seminars or sessions that are old hat; seek out opportunities to be exposed to something new. Attend every social event. You don't have to stay until the bitter end of every dinner or party; just be sure to take advantage of every chance to make an impression and to connect. And try to stay in the hotel where the conference is being held. It's easier to get to every event, and you'll be more likely to reinforce connections with people you meet because you'll run into them in a variety of situations.

▶ Participate actively. Ask questions, make comments, introduce yourself to speakers and conference coordinators. Share

COME TO THE FAIR

Another great but underutilized opportunity to represent your company and add visible, quantifiable value is to participate in recruitment efforts. Get friendly with someone in HR and volunteer to attend recruiting fairs. Playing the enthusiastic, informed employee at a recruiting fair can help attract desirable job candidates to your company. You'll get bonus points when a hot prospect tells your boss he decided to join your team because he was impressed with how you represented the company culture and experience. Double-bonus points, maybe.

your business card and collect business cards. But remember, it's not a contest of who can collect the most cards. It's a challenge to come home with one killer card—and for *yours* to be the killer card someone else takes back to *his* Rolodex.

▶ Stretch yourself socially. Believe it or not, a room full of strangers is the *best* place to improve your people skills. You have nothing to lose and everything to gain by behaving with ease, especially if it doesn't come naturally. Go out of your way to introduce yourself to anyone, everyone. Act like a gracious host by bringing others into conversations, making introductions, helping other people connect. Accept invitations. However cocooned you may be back home, now you're the butterfly.

▶ Finally, bring home the booty. Write a short e-mail report for your boss and other relevant parties summarizing the practical takeaway and/or industry news. If you learned a new skill or were exposed to an innovative concept, offer to share it with your team. And look for a way—right away—to apply what you learned to improve your own work. Make sure your boss sees it happen. *That* makes the best bulletproof impression of all.

▶▶▶ *Use conferences to practice your professional pitch.*
▶▶▶ *Network like crazy.*
▶▶▶ *Make a great impression for yourself and your company.*

9. FIND A MENTOR

Everyone needs a mentor. You need one if you're new on the job, if you're in over your head, if you're stagnating in your job, even if you're excelling in your job. A good mentor can give you valuable day-to-day guidance, help you solve problems, and protect you when bullets are flying. Of course, a *bad* mentor can give you harmful advice, make your problems worse, and bring you down with his sinking ship. So find a good mentor, okay?

Start by figuring out what you need. If you're struggling in your job, you want to hook up with someone who has solid experience in your area, good instincts, and the time and desire to give you the support you need. If you're doing well, you'll benefit from working with someone who has followed a career path similar to the one you desire and who will be generous in helping you grow your career. In either case, you need to have a very clear idea of what you want to improve about your performance or work experience. A mentor's not a buddy or confidant; he's a partner in helping you get from A to B to C and so on. You need to know where *you* want to go before you ask someone to help you get there.

An ideal mentor is someone whose advice and intelligence you respect, whom you can trust to be honest with you, and with whom you feel you can communicate freely. At the same time, you want your mentor to be further enough along in her career than you are that you can really benefit from her experience and her well-informed and constructive criticism.

TRUE STORY

Shelley was a young, smart up-and-comer in a slick political consulting firm. She was also very attractive and sensitive to what she perceived as jealousy or resentment toward her on the part of the older female partners in the firm. If Shelley had been smart, she would have courted one of those women to be a mentor, turning her from an opponent into an advocate. Instead, she worked around them and solicited support from the male managers and partners when she needed it. When the firm lost a big account that Shelley had been working on, she lost her job. Without a single vote of support for keeping her from the women partners, she didn't stand a chance.

Potential mentors are often people you work with whom you gravitate toward naturally. They're likable, smart, and generous. You admire what they've accomplished and feel comfortable around them. They may not be in your immediate work group or even in your department. But you like they way they operate and feel as if you could learn from them. So the question is, how to get the whole mentor-mentee thing going?

Sometimes it just happens organically, without any formal arrangement or acknowledgement. You just fall into a relationship, and it works just the way it's supposed to without anyone saying a word. Other times it's appropriate to come out and ask someone if she'd be willing to be a mentor. Because there's a time commitment involved, it's only fair to bring it to a conscious level. It's not as if you're asking her to go steady or anything. It's just an informal agreement that you need help and she's going to make the time to give it to you.

Some companies even have a formal mentor program, where

WHAT A MENTOR SHOULD BE

▶ Honest and trustworthy

▶ Committed

▶ A good role model

▶ An effective communicator and motivator

▶ Convinced of your potential

executives and managers are assigned to entry-level employees to help them acclimate to the company's culture and expectations. This is more like the faculty advisor arrangement you had in college or even like a sponsor in AA—an obligation to both parties rather than an option. But it's still useful for establishing a valuable contact at a higher level in the company.

Once you have a mentor relationship, take good care of it. Set up a regular date for coffee with your mentor. Keep him apprised of your progress, challenges, and questions. Run ideas past him, vent your frustrations (within reason), and ask for advice on how to deal with them. Be sure every exchange isn't about some giant problem or frantic crisis; your mentor is there to help nurture you in your job and career, not just to help you put out fires. That said, do call her daily for advice in panicky times. When bullets start flying around the office, this is the person who can tell you when to duck or fire back.

If you turn out to be a successful mentee—you're learning, advancing, and maturing, thanks in part to your mentor's guidance—your mentor can be a powerful advocate for you when opportunities or challenges arise in the future.

▶▶▶ *Think of a mentor as someone who can help guide you through the minefields at work.*

▶▶▶ *Find a mentor who will be an effective ally and supporter.*

10. TALK TO YOUR BOSS

You'd be surprised how many people go out of their way to avoid talking to their bosses. Maybe he's not the world's easiest person to talk to or he's not very responsive or helpful. Or maybe you're not very confident communicating with someone in a position of authority over you. Either way, it's *your* problem, not *his* and here's the bulletproof truth: If you don't have a regular course of communication with your boss, when it's time to trim staff, you'll be just a body in a chair with a big bull's-eye on your back.

The onus is on you to establish a pattern and style of communication between you and your boss that works for both of you. And that doesn't revolve just around problems; you'll both dread talking to each other if you do so only when bombs are going off. Communication is the key to purposefully cultivating the chemistry with your boss that will make or break your job.

Chemistry comes from successful one-on-one contact and eye contact. That's all there is to making an emotional connection with your boss. That lets him know you are a *person*, not just a colleague or a subordinate. In careful, discreet ways, show him who you are—talk about your family, your interests, sports, movies, whatever. These are your human connectors. Your chemistry with your boss has to be strong—I like to describe it as almost but not quite romantic, because there's a sort of a dance to building the relationship that's similar to romance. If you're smart,

BODY LANGUAGE

You say as much with your body as you do with your words. So be fluent. Keep your head up, and, while this is a point I repeatedly make, I can't stress enough the importance of making steady, direct eye contact. Stand or sit with your shoulders back and with overall good posture. Don't cross your legs, but do keep your hands on your lap or by your sides, not on your hips and never crossed over your chest. Folding your arms suggests inaccessibility and arrogance—not to mention that it makes you look fat. Finally, speak slowly and clearly. This sends a message of confidence, competence, and control.

you constantly find ways to magnetize the relationship so that when troubles come, he fires someone else instead of you.

First, figure out the most effective way to communicate. It'll be some combination of e-mail, phone, memos, and face-to-face, depending on your boss's style and the nature of the information you need to exchange. Even if he's a 99 percent electronic communicator, you need to make a point of engaging in regular in-person dialogue. It's still the only way to make an emotional connection and to be sure he knows who you really are. It's also the least likely to be misconstrued, which happens with e-mail and voice mail all the time. Use electronic communication to confirm verbal communication, never as a primary means of communication if you can help it. And skip texting and social networking connections altogether. That's for you and your friends, not you and your boss.

N.B. There are some bosses who *prefer* to keep communication clinical and electronic, versus human and in person. You're not going to change them, so working as effectively with this style as you can is the best way to play it bulletproof.

Always be prepared for a conversation with your boss. Have an agenda and a point of view. Be ready to think on your feet. Be ready to accept criticism. Do ask questions, but don't let the whole conversation seem like one big question mark. Be positive and in control of your emotions. Showing anger never works out well, and weeping tends not to put you in the best light, either. Put up a firm, unemotional front with the kind of boss who tends to tirade instead of talk. And be sensitive to timing; delivering bad news or asking for a raise while he's running out the door late for a meeting doesn't usually work out very well.

Keep him apprised of what you're doing. A long memo about how you cleaned up your contact database isn't necessary; a

TAMING THE TIGER

Communicating with a difficult or demanding boss can be challenging. And this cat isn't going to change its stripes. Adapt a strategy and techniques that allow you to communicate effectively no matter what. Be professional. Don't show emotion, and don't take anything personally. Stick to a simple agenda, and try to control the tenor of the conversation by being measured and direct. Follow up with a short e-mail confirmation of the outcome of your conversation, taking a very neutral, matter-of-fact tone. This will remind your boss of the content of your conversation, and it will give you a little electronic paper trail of what went down, just in case. Remember: You can have productive communication and even a good and valuable relationship with a difficult boss. You just need to take the tiger by the tail.

JUST SO YOU KNOW

On the one hand, crying has no place at work. On the other, if you have to cry for leverage in a critical situation, do it. I'm not talking about daily waterworks. I'm talking about the rare but very effective revelation to your boss that you're human, as a way of strengthening your personal connection and, frankly, for getting what you need. A dispensation for missing two important days of work because your father is gravely ill? Cry. A pass for getting chewed out by your boss for being chronically late? Don't cry. Just say you're sorry and quit being late, for God's sake.

once-a-month, brief, bulleted accounting of short- and long-term accomplishments and future goals is a way to keep him conscious of your contributions and your progress.

▶▶▶ *Cultivate good chemistry with your boss by establishing effective communication.*
▶▶▶ *Control the tenor and content of communication with your boss.*

11. GROW YOUR CIRCLE

This is going to sound very junior high, but it's crucial to hang out with the right people at work. While on the one hand you can never have too many friends, on the other there's only so much time to spend on the people in your work life, so make sure they're smart, well dressed, and well thought of by their peers and supervisors. Your "crew" should be highly presentable and ambitious up-and-comers, not unkempt sloths. The idea is to have a network of valuable professional friendships that can help you bulletproof your career, not sabotage it. So build a team of top-drawer allies across the organization who make you look good—and who can do you as many favors as you should be prepared to do for them.

You usually have three sets of friends at work—the real friends, the professional friends, and the frienemies.

Real friends are the ones you genuinely like and with whom you'd choose to hang out even if they were not your coworkers. These are usually the friends you meet during your first week of work and who make up the little circle from which you hardly stray. You eat lunch together, you have drinks together, you gripe

REMEMBER NAMES!

Pay attention when someone tells you his name. Better yet, be genuinely interested in his name. If you glean nothing else from the conversation, make *sure* you know the person's name after you've said good night. Usually we're so busy thinking about ourselves and what we want to say that we forget to pay attention to the other guy. Here's a three-step process for recalling someone's name:

1. See number 4, "Listen up."

2. Repeat the name to yourself once or twice. Sometimes it helps to imagine writing the name. Use the name frequently while you converse. Or confirm his name when you part ways. "Jim, right? It was nice to meet you."

3. Write down the person's name as soon as you can, as well as anything you can remember about what he does or any other identifying features. The first name is the main thing. If you get to know her better, you can move on to her eight-syllable Czechoslovakian surname.

THE ANATOMY OF A PROFESSIONAL FRIEND

A professional friend isn't someone whom you pay to be your friend, although I have some ideas on how to start *that* business (perhaps that's the next book). It's someone who's your friend in a professional context versus a personal one. A good professional friend:

▶ Shares your goals at work. Both of you should desire to learn, grow, advance, and support each other—and hang on to your jobs.

▶ Shows discretion. Though you should never share details about your personal life or opinions about your work life that could be damaging to you if made public, you should be able to trust each other and hold each other's confidence. Take time to be sure of the level of confidence you can share, though. It's one thing to commiserate about the department assistant refusing to answer the phone; it's another to pass along privileged information about what you're working on. Use your head; know what's harmless poop you can share to make you closer and what's best kept to yourself to protect your job.

▶ Understands the parameters of your professional relationship. It's collegial, not emotional or deeply affectionate. And if it goes beyond collegial and turns sexual, it's no longer a professional friendship, it's an office romance. Beware. And see number 18, "Behave appropriately."

together about obnoxious colleagues or a tough boss. It's comforting to have a close social unit, but it's much more important to have a comprehensive network of friends on the job. These are your professional friends.

Friendships across the organization can be a powerful source of support in good times and bad, providing access to inside information, useful feedback about your own performance, and invaluable assistance in future job hunts. These relationships also give a strong perception of your being well liked, well rounded, and well connected, which can make all the difference in the world when axes are falling all around you.

To build a network of professional friends, you have to get out of your cube and reach out to people around you whom you haven't paid attention to before, as well as to others who are well beyond your immediate work group. Make a point of getting to know one new person a week, even if it's just introducing yourself in the elevator or sitting next to him in the cafeteria. Ask about his job, what projects he's working on. Try to sustain the connection by following up with an e-mail or phone call. And if nothing else, *remember his name.* People are flattered when they see you again and you remember their names; it's almost always the beginning of a beautiful friendship.

Look for opportunities to attend events where many departments of your company are represented. The holiday party and the company picnic are obvious, but not always the best places to make connections that stick. In-house conferences, training sessions, outside speaker events—these are great chances to meet and mingle with your farther-flung coworkers. Make a goal of having at least one friendly contact in every department of your company and loads of them throughout the company in support positions. The boss's secretary or the guys in the copy center may be able to do you a big favor some day. Have a friend in "corporate," even if headquarters is a thousand miles away from where you work. Make friends long distance if you have to, by telephone or e-mail. Have a friend in HR, even if he's just the benefits person. You always need a friend in HR. All of these professional relationships—from the corporate counsel you met

JUST SO YOU KNOW

You never know whether your most valuable professional friendship is going to be with the senior vice president you got to know when you discovered you both had Labradoodles or the hip-hop kid who runs the copy center. The most important professional friend I have is my longtime and trusted assistant, Sean. He's extremely loyal and very private, and, most important, he's a lot smarter than I am. He is protective of my interests, but he's not an ass kisser, and he knows that's exactly what I need. He's not afraid to call me out when I'm dead wrong, but he always does it privately. He respects my authority, and we learn from each other. Truth be told, though, I learn much more from him than he does from me.

playing outfield at the company picnic to a kid in the mailroom—will be invaluable to you in the long *and* short terms.

Finally, you have your frienemies. These are the ones whom you don't really like very much and who may be somewhat outwardly competitive with you, but who are most certainly your rivals—especially when it comes to whose job is bulletproof or not. You need to keep these folks on your radar, and being an out-and-out enemy doesn't allow the proximity you need to keep an eye on them. So as Tony Soprano might say, keep your friends close but your frienemies closer. Maintain a cordial, collegial, careful relationship with every one of them.

Here is the heartwarming part of the whole picture of your circle of friends: In my opinion, high-quality professional friendships in the workplace result in higher productivity, a generally more positive and creative outlook, and greater longevity. That's right. Having good friends at work makes you happier and more effective in your job and therefore more likely to keep it. So make more friends.

▶▶▶ *Have the right friends.*
▶▶▶ *Cultivate professional friendships that will benefit you.*

12. INTRODUCE YOURSELF

Unless you work for a small business, it's unlikely that you'll ever have the occasion to work side by side with the president, CEO, or chairman of the board of your company. They're many layers removed from you, and so far, that's worked out just fine, right? You just keep chipping away at the work on your desk, hoping to make a few vertical moves on the organizational chart before all is said and done. And they're out there in the stratosphere, making the big decisions, taking the big risks. Better them than you, no?

One of the biggest mistakes you can make is thinking there's no connection between you and the Big Boss. The fact is, you have two huge things in common: you both work for the same company, and you both want the company to succeed. Oh, and there's a third thing: you both want to hang on to your jobs! That's right. The higher-ups are just as concerned as you are about being bulletproof, maybe more so. The targets on their foreheads are bigger than the one on yours. When you start thinking of them as leaders in a battle you're all fighting at once, the distance between you shrinks a little, doesn't it?

You can use this important fact you have in common to help secure your own position in a very simple way: introduce yourself. You don't need to get your name on a billboard to make yourself known to a company bigwig. You just need to find an opportunity to say hello and accomplish three things: say your

YOUR PERSONAL PITCH

You should always have your personal pitch ready to roll off your tongue, and not just to your bosses. It's the thirty-second advertisement you must have on hand at all times to market yourself to anyone. It's your self-sell, and it's how you express, reinforce, and extend your own brand.

Your personal pitch should explain who you are, what you do, and how you add unique value to your company and/or your clients in clear, confident, and succinct language. To create your pitch, make a list of your two or three most impressive credentials and your top two accomplishments in your job. Create a little you-in-a-nutshell that combines your identifying information (name, position) with your selling information (that swanky college you attended, the award-winning work you've done, how much money you've saved/made for the company, a great project you're working on, etc.). You're not bragging here, just trying to convey your own top selling points as concisely as you can.

When you have a smart, tight, compelling pitch down pat, practice it in the mirror until you know it inside and out and can do it without sounding as if you've practiced at all. Use it when you meet people in high places, use it at conferences, use it at parties. It's like a business card on steroids.

name, assert your connection to her, and share your personal pitch.

I'm not suggesting you try to become BFFs with the CEO. You're not trying to leapfrog to the upper echelons, à la corporate movie fairy tales like *Working Girl* or *Big*. You're aiming to help the higher-ups help *you* bulletproof your job. And they won't even know they're doing it.

First, make yourself familiar with the names, faces, and responsibilities of the folks in high places. Start with your company directory and then Google the hell out of each of them. You want the front story, the back story, and everything in between. Why all the sleuthing? At the least you'll be up to date on whatever they're doing that's in the news, which can be a valuable starter to your introductory conversation. At the most, you might find out he attended the same college as you did or he comes from the same small town as your granddad, in which case you've hit the mother lode. Such personal details are very powerful connectors that can multiply the value of a simple introduction dramatically.

Next, brainstorm opportunities for you to introduce yourself. Identify company or outside events these people attend. Ideally, you'll turn up at a professional gathering where you get to make your introduction *and* make a good impression by being in attendance at a top-drawer event. Your opportunity could also come in the form of a chance three-minute elevator ride together, however, so be ready at all times.

Your mother was right when she told you that you don't get a second chance to make a first impression, so once you get your chance, nail it. Say your name, make your connection, and serve up your personal pitch. Make it smooth and make it snappy, in-

ASK YOURSELF:

▶ What do I do?

▶ What do I specialize in?

▶ What is extraordinary about the work I do?

▶ What is extraordinary about my background?

▶ What has been my greatest accomplishment?

THE VIAGRA HANDSHAKE

Having a bad handshake is like introducing yourself with a piece of spinach in your teeth or a gaping hole in the seam of your pants. It's hard to ignore and leaves a long-lasting impression. And not the good kind. I think of a good, hearty handshake as a Viagra handshake, for all the reasons you'd imagine. Here's what a Viagra handshake is like:

► Firm: Not Incredible Hulk firm, but firm enough that you convey your confidence, capability, and trustworthiness. Ask friends and family to give you honest feedback on the firmness of your handshake. Women especially need to offer a firm handshake and should be offered them as well, particularly by men.

► Perpendicular: Palm down sends an aggressive, dominant message, while palm up sends a weak, submissive message. Shake so that your hand is parallel to the other person's.

► Brief: A handshake is not a pumping contest. One-Mississippi, two-Mississippi is plenty long enough.

Be the first to offer a handshake and say your full name at the same time, even in a situation where you may have met the person before. And make eye contact. If you don't engage in eye contact when you shake someone's hand, you come off at best as insecure and at worst as shifty.

Bill Clinton is the master of the Viagra handshake and eye contact. Every time he shakes someone's hand, he looks the person in the eye and gently touches the person's right elbow with his left hand. This makes the connection personal, makes the person feel he is enjoying his full and enthusiastic attention. Giving someone "The Clinton" is a great way to close a deal.

JUST SO YOU KNOW

Name-dropping is a nifty tool when you're trying to make a connection with the Big Boss. There's a fine art to it, though, so do it with caution. If you've researched the boss and discovered you know someone in common (your college roommate was the son of his first boss, for example), find a pleasant way to drop that fact into conversation. If you know someone notable in your field you feel confident would impress him, go ahead and mention it. Be absolutely sure, though; you don't want to bring up someone who's his mortal enemy or something. And drop a person's name only once; more than that makes you look like an overeager amateur. Skillful name-dropping works like a charm; ham-handed name-dropping can peg you as a moron, a braggart, or both.

cluding one fact he might remember, such as a notable project you worked on or where you went to school. Be prepared to answer a question or two about yourself and to ask a question about something you discovered in your research, if appropriate, in order to shift the conversation back to him. Avoid obsequiousness ("I've read all your books!") in favor of being interested and well informed ("I understand you have a new book coming out"). Asking whether he has kids, where he went to college, or what his hometown is is pretty safe, especially when you've done your homework and you already know the answers.

Follow up with an e-mail or a handwritten note, reminding him of your brief meeting and saying how much you enjoyed it. Reiterate your connection to him, and note something that happened or was said that will anchor the exchange in his memory ("It was a pleasure to meet you, and I look forward to reading your new book"). This will increase the chance that the next time you see him, he'll remember that he met *you*.

Repeat this process with as many upper-management types as you can without becoming known as an executive stalker. And find a way to carefully, casually, seamlessly mention these meetings to your immediate supervisors. This kind of strategic name-dropping is money in the bulletproof bank; it creates a subtle perception of you as being more connected (and more protected) than perhaps you really are.

▶▶▶ ***Make a connection with the Big Bosses.***
▶▶▶ ***Be prepared to make a memorable impression.***
▶▶▶ ***Master the Viagra handshake.***

13. PUBLICIZE YOUR ACCOMPLISHMENTS

There's a trick to making sure the right people know what you're doing right. On the one hand, you don't want to be perceived as a credit hog or a braggart. On the other, if you don't tell people about your successes and accomplishments, no one else will. So how can you toot your own horn without making too much noise?

First of all, find a way to make your message "we" instead of "me." Consider how your accomplishment has benefited your colleagues and the company at large. Example: An e-mail to your department manager or a division executive might say, "Thought you'd like to know that my team just completed Project X, and I'm pleased to report that we not only came in on time and under budget but also that the client has asked us to take on Project Y." Making it "we" news helps ensure that your boss won't feel threatened by your accomplishments.

GOOD NEWS THAT'S FIT TO PRINT

Sometimes the best way to get your news out there is to make sure it's black and white and read all over. Some kinds of information are better suited to this approach than others. An example of a printworthy news item includes a project that benefits the community or a particular charity. Or, more objectively, you might be part of a study or a project that could generate good PR for your company. If you think you have a news nugget, go right to your company's communications department (hopefully you've already made friends with the communications director or her assistant so that your item is handled expeditiously). If your company is big enough, it's someone's job to get the firm's name in the news, and you might be handing them a juicy item on a silver platter. You look good, they look good, everybody wins. Whether your name is mentioned in the press release and news article or not, make high-quality copies or scans and send around with a cover note to your "Thought you'd like to know . . ." list. Don't rush to the AP with your latest news, however; first find out what your company's protocol is regarding the media, and follow it to a T.

Better yet, get someone else (such as your immediate supervisor) to pass along the news by e-mail or through a company newsletter. You'll get the same exposure but with a little more value because someone is tooting your horn *for* you. You can also send around a "Good job" e-mail to a broader audience. Your sharing the news implies your ownership of the group accomplishment.

Make friends with the person in charge of the company newsletter. After all the hot scoops about blood drives and benefits, these publications usually run out of content. When you work for a big company, the CEO or president doesn't always show up at the holiday party. But he *always* reads his own company's

TRUE STORY

Ryan, a junior accountant in a big accounting firm, had been a long-distance runner since high school and frequently competed in local and regional races on the weekends. When he won a 10K fund-raising race for cancer, he sent an FYI e-mail to his company's PR director, thinking it might turn up in the monthly newsletter. Instead, a nice mention in the local newspaper caught the attention of the company president, who had lost a brother to cancer. She e-mailed Ryan, and before he knew it, he was on a first-name basis with the Big Boss and wearing his company's logo on his race jerseys.

newsletter. So never miss a chance to get your news into the company newsletter.

Use any opportunity to share recent successes in person; create a thirty-second sound bite to casually pass along to colleagues in the elevator, at lunch, in meetings. This will help spread your good news in house the old-fashioned way—by word of mouth. Make a habit of sharing your accomplishments like this so that there's a steady hum of good buzz about you.

Finally, prepare a summary of your accomplishments to submit in advance of any kind of job review or progress report meeting. This front-loads the exchange with your quantifiable and valuable contributions, putting you at a bulletproof advantage.

▶ ▶ ▶ *Don't be shy about letting others know your good news.*

14. BE A FAN

If you hate your job or you hate your boss or you hate the company you work for, chances are that both your coworkers and your boss know it. Your misery makes you toxic, and while you may be a tolerable, necessary evil when times are good, it's unlikely anything will protect your job during a rough patch. That's the hard truth of it.

If, however, you're basically content with your lot (and I'm assuming that since you're reading this book you are), you need to ramp that up by several degrees, from blithely satisfied employee to full-blown company fan. That's right, the kind that wears the team colors painted on his face and waves around a big "We're #1" foam finger.

There are two simple reasons why you need to drink the company Kool-Aid. First, being a fan is the opposite of being a miserable malcontent, a workplace character who has a big fat "Fire me" sign on his back on a good day. Second, when you behave like a fan—genuinely rooting for your company, your colleagues, and your clients to succeed—your bosses will notice your posi-

ASK YOURSELF:

► Do I speak well of my company to colleagues?

► Do I speak well of my company to strangers?

► Am I happy when my company succeeds?

► Do I let my colleagues know I'm rooting for their success?

► Am I a positive influence on my coworkers?

tive attitude and they'll *really* notice how it improves morale all around. Attitude trumps qualifications any day of the week. At the end of the day, the enthusiasm you conjure up for your job and your company may be your most valuable weapon in safeguarding your employment.

When you genuinely root for your team, rather than being indifferent or, worse, cynical, the positive energy spreads to your coworkers and in turn spreads to your boss. Your energy and optimism can be a shot in the arm for everyone and during tough times can change the work climate from malaise to excitement. Your attitude makes you bulletproof and even gives you a leg up when promotion time rolls around.

▶▶▶ **Look for ways to show that you're the company's biggest booster.**

BULLETPROOF TAKEAWAY

Becoming visible doesn't happen overnight. And because *The Office* is truth, not fiction, some of us—the awkward Dwight Schrutes, for example—have a bigger challenge than others—say, the likable Jim Halperts—in pulling it off. But *anyone* can begin raising and improving his profile right now. Here's what you can do:

▶ Focus on the stuff you can control—your work habits and your appearance, for example.

▶ Reach for the low-hanging fruit of longer-term tasks that best apply to your situation—say, offer-

YOU'RE NOT SIMON COWELL

The irascible star of *American Idol* is paid a boatload of money to be pissy, disagreeable, and insulting. You are not. Besides his giant paycheck, the biggest difference between you and Simon is that he's playing a role and you're playing yourself. You may think of your grouchy candor as straight shooting and your litanies of others' shortcomings as constructive criticism, but your coworkers hate it and they probably hate you, too.

Simon can afford not to care if people hate him, but you can't. Work is a popularity contest, and the harsh truth is that when jobs are being cut, the guy who keeps his job is the one the boss likes the best. And he's usually the friendly guy, the pleasant guy, the guy who makes people comfortable, not miserable. So next time you're tempted to say to a colleague, "That was like embarrassingly atrocious karaoke"—don't.

if necessary criticism follows: "It's great we made our deadline, but we probably made a few too many mistakes." Speak as "we," not as "you," in order to keep criticism from becoming personal. And think before you speak, even rehearse what you're going to say before you say it. You can't take back a snide or hurtful remark, but you *can* stop yourself from making it in the first place. Finally, don't ever try to make yourself look smart at someone else's expense. Correcting a colleague in front of everyone for misusing or mispronouncing a word will just confirm that you're as big an asshole everyone probably already thinks you are.

▶ Pay attention to your tone of voice. Shouting is never a good idea, of course, but neither is sarcasm or condescension, which has as much to do with *how* you say something as *what* you say. Think of your tone of voice as the tune and your words as the lyrics. This helps you remember to try to sing a pleasant song.

▶ Be tactful. Timing is everything when it comes to playing nicely at work. Never rag on someone else in front of others; if you need to confront a coworker about a problem, do it privately and thoughtfully. Be sensitive to the state of mind of the other person; your boss doesn't need an earful from you when he's just gotten a dressing down from his own boss. Neither does the guy in the cube next door when he's killing himself to meet a deadline.

▶▶▶ **Be careful of what you say and how you say it at work.**
▶▶▶ **Show tact and sensitivity when communicating with colleagues.**

17. LEAVE YOUR PROBLEMS AT HOME

Have you hit a bumpy spot in your marriage? Are your kids acting out? Are you worried about your ailing mother? Are you having trouble making your mortgage payment? Well, welcome to everyone's world. We're *all* stressed and pressed and pinched and terrified about lots of things, and it can be hard to keep all of those personal problems from spilling over at work. But the fact is, if you can't find a way to leave your problems at home, you may end up with *no* work.

People who drag their personal baggage to work do it for a lot of reasons. Some consider their coworkers their friends and see no reason not to share the details of their private lives. Others are so weighed down by personal trials that their general mood and productivity are diminished, which invariably affects the people around them. Still others are drama queens who aren't happy unless there's some bit of commotion around them, per-

JUST SO YOU KNOW

In a perfect world, you would be the picture of professionalism and no one you work with would ever know what a wreck your personal life is. In the real world, though, there are times when blabbing about your problem to your boss is the *only* way you're going to bulletproof your job.

Part of the ongoing "romance" with your boss is getting to know her—and letting her get to know you—just enough that you care (a little) about what's going on in each other's lives. And though you never want your problems to define you or distract from your contribution, sometimes the very careful revelation of a problem to your boss can help you.

An example of being careful: If your boss doesn't have children, she can't relate to people's kid problems and will have no patience for yours. So keep those problems to yourself. On the other hand, if you know she's a dog lover and you, too, have a dog, it's a bit of personal common ground that can come in handy.

An example of how revealing a problem can help you: Everything in your life is in disarray, your kid is flunking geometry, the furnace needs to be replaced, and your dog has some kind of lump on his neck that might be bad. Tell the boss about the dog's lump. Then use the tiny window of sympathy and slack she gives you over it to swiftly deal with that and all your other issues. And by the way: when you make your appeal, be direct and unemotional. When you grovel or simper or beg for a favor, you look weak *and* problematic.

Warning: You get only a couple of "Get out of jail free" sympathy cards from your superiors. So use them very, very judiciously and only when you have plenty of goodwill in the bank. Otherwise they'll figure out real quick that you and your problems are a problem for them.

sonal or professional. All of these people need to leave the bags at home.

When you share all your personal problems in the workplace, you begin to look like one big problem to everyone around you. Flat tires, sick kids, a root canal, a broken dishwasher, a death in the family, a flooded basement, a cheating boyfriend, chronic migraines, blah, blah, blah. If you make the mistake of sharing just one problem just one time with just one coworker, you crack open the door to your personal life and make yourself vulnerable to judgment, indiscretion, or worse. If you talk about all your problems all the time, you create a perception of yourself as being plagued, overwrought, unlucky, and even incompetent. If you can't handle the minutiae of your personal life, how can you handle that big Henderson account?

Keep the personal stuff away from the professional stuff by being very strict with yourself about what you share with coworkers. When you're going through a difficult time, stick to neutral subjects (sports, movies, cooking) to fill the conversational space that might otherwise be claimed by their nosy questions and your overly detailed answers.

Find another place to park your personal problems. Hit the gym, volunteer at an animal shelter, take a cooking class, whatever. Using professional relationships for catharsis makes you an emotional burden to others or, worse, a crackpot.

Be proactive. If you need help resolving your problems, get it from a doctor, a counselor, a minister/priest/rabbi/imam, a lawyer, an accountant, a mechanic, a hairdresser—whoever can give you the support you need and help you make a plan for addressing your problems before it's too late. Don't let it get so bad that your supervisor is forced to confront you about changes he's observing in your attitude or productivity. If that happens, HR may

JUST SO YOU KNOW

"Work-life balance" is something most people managed to accomplish for generations without needing a special word to describe it: get up, go to work, do your job, come home, eat dinner, walk the dog, mow the lawn, go to sleep, get up, go to work again. What's changed is another word that's crept into our modern vocabulary: "stress." It appears that we've become slaves to our jobs and the attendant pressure is affecting our health, our relationships with family and friends, and the general quality of our lives. In short, we're burning ourselves out, and there's a whole movement afoot demanding that we make work-life balance a workplace priority by instituting stress management programs, time management techniques, and even shorter or flexible hours.

Let me tell you something. Stress is a dangerous word you should never say out loud at work. It's just another way of saying "I can't handle this job, so you might as well fire me." Look. It's not called "relaxation" or "leisure," it's called "work." Work is hard, and though it can be immensely enjoyable, it's mostly just work. Sniveling about how stressed you are just makes you look incompetent to do your job. An emergency room technician or a fighter pilot—*those* people have stressful jobs. But if either one of them went around talking about how "stressed out" he or she was, how long do you think it would be before that person would have to look for a new job?

Please understand: I'm all for balance. But I guarantee that there are few things that will make you feel more stressed—and *unbalanced*—than losing your job. Losing a job is right up there with death and divorce on the stress-o-meter. So don't. Instead of letting your relationships suffer *because* of your work, take care of your relationships on an ongoing basis so your personal network can help you tend to your needs and problems when they arise. Similarly, if you habitually take care of your health by eating well, exercising, and sleeping enough, your health will be your ally instead of your enemy during difficult times on the job.

refer you to an Employee Assistance Program (EAP), which is a company-sponsored counseling service. Your employer may *tell you* he's happy to see you getting the help you need, but now HR has a record of your problem on file, and while technically your employer can't use that against you, it'll still have a perception of your being troubled. Though some EAPs are strictly confidential—an external resource is made available and the company is never advised when an employee makes use of it—be smart about how you deal with personal issues and how you choose the people in whom you confide.

If you're really struggling with personal matters, think of work as a refuge from your nonwork problems. Really. When things are a wreck in your personal life, the structure and methodical accomplishments of day-to-day work can be like medicine. If your job is the one part of your life that's not giving you

TRUE STORY

Vic owned a medium-sized electronics business that suffered a big hit in the recession of the early 1990s, and he made a decision to dip into the company's pension plan to save the business. Several employees quit during this time and were entitled to be paid their full pension benefits, which, of course, were not available. The employees could have filed charges against him, but they didn't, mostly because he told them he was in treatment for prostate cancer and needed more time to sort things out. Playing the personal tragedy card this one critical time bought him time to borrow money, pay back the pension fund, save his ass, and save his company. That's not an everyday way of doing business—in fact, it's a Machiavellian approach ordinary folks can't get away with too often, if at all—but sometimes you do what you have to do.

grief, hug it like a life raft. And make keeping it your number-one priority.

▶ ▶ ▶ *Keep your personal problems to yourself.*

▶ ▶ ▶ *Don't let your private issues make your work suffer.*

18. BEHAVE APPROPRIATELY

Strangely, one of the most common ways people get themselves into trouble at work is also the easiest to avoid. Every time you "cross the line" by getting into a heated conversation with co-workers about George Bush or Jesus or making others uncomfortable with your off-color jokes or blue-streak cursing or hitting on that adorable receptionist—again—you draw negative attention to yourself on the job. Add to that racial insensitivity, careless sexual innuendo, and other kinds of not-very-funny baiting, and you're just one harassment complaint from the unemployment line.

If you're the kind of person who regularly makes these sorts of mistakes, you probably don't much care whether people think badly of you. "I am what I am," as Popeye would say. Well, spinach won't help Popeye a damn bit if he's loaded up his personnel file with these kinds of senseless, stupid infractions.

Work isn't where you exercise your First Amendment rights to say whatever you want and to "be yourself." It's where you *behave yourself.* It's where you stay inside the lines of good decorum, not cross them. It's where you are above reproach in what you say to your colleagues at all times. It's where you bend over backward to do the unimpeachable right thing and avoid at all

THE DOWN AND DIRTY ABOUT OFFICE ROMANCE

If you flipped straight to this page to find out if it's okay to have sex with someone you work with, you're probably not going to like what I have to say. I have long been a cheerful supporter of office romance, in part because so many successful relationships get their start in the workplace. Is there a bond stronger than a common livelihood? And what's more attractive than career ambition? Please. All that time together and closeness and chemistry—who needs Match.com?

And let's be honest, it seems kind of futile to try to stand in the way of animal attraction and raging hormones in the close quarters of the office. But if your primary objective is to bulletproof your job, you should undertake a romantic or sexual relationship with a coworker with extreme caution. Here's why:

If (or, rather, *when)* your coworkers discover your relationship, you will become fodder for runaway gossip. The only thing you ever want discussed about you is what great work you do, not who you're doing.

If your boss finds out what you're up to, she's likely to make a negative judgment about your lack of judgment, especially if intraoffice fraternization is forbidden or frowned upon by your company. If you're lucky, your superiors will shrug and say you're "only human." If you're not so lucky, they'll assume you lack self-control or you're more interested in your sex life than your job. Or worse, they'll throw the employee handbook at you

costs doing the actionable wrong thing. And finally, it's where you try to make loyal friends, not mortal enemies.

Most big companies (and lots of small ones) have an employee handbook that includes Standard Operating Procedures and a Code of Ethics that makes crystal clear what kind of behavior is expected and what is strictly forbidden in the work-

and give you the boot. In any case, you come off looking worse, not better, than you did before they knew this about you, which hardly strengthens your bulletproof position when your job is on the line.

Finally, if the relationship goes south while you're still working together, those familiar residual bad feelings will make it really hard for both of you to do your best at work. Collaborating on projects will be difficult, shared professional friendships will be compromised, and if one of you is angry enough (hell hath no fury, etc.), things can go postal on a dime.

Multiply all of the above by about 100 if your intraoffice entanglement is with your boss. Sexy? Yes. Exciting? Definitely. Worth it? Probably not. Unless, of course, you're in the generally regrettable situation where sleeping with your boss is helping you keep your job. Hey, I'm sure not telling you to do that. But I'm not telling you not to, either.

I'm all for bodice-ripping passion, and I'll admit that some of the best romantic relationships I have had have been with coworkers. Sometimes love (and lust) simply will not be denied. Just be very clear about the risk involved. Let's just say that it's not the world's best bulletproofing behavior.

If wild horses can't stop you from rolling around with a coworker, do not discuss it with anyone. Anyone! If you and your little friend can keep your escapades to yourself, it's possible they might not come back and bite you in the ass. That's a big if, of course. And a big might.

place. When you accept a job, you're usually asked to sign a form indicating that you've read and agree to abide by the SOP and employee handbook. These documents are like the constitution of the company and reflect its culture. So if you don't like the culture you see there, don't sign the form and don't take the job. Period. Work is not a democracy.

And beyond all those rules written in black and white, there are unspoken rules that have to do with the culture of the company and the specific individuals with whom you work. These are "rules" such as don't drink at office functions if your boss is a teetotaler and other use-your-head stuff like that.

Listen, you're trying to bulletproof yourself. So even though I shouldn't have to spell it out because I'm *sure* you were raised better than this, I'm going to remind you of some simple rules that may help you save your job: Keep your big mouth shut. Avoid subjects including race, religion, politics, sex, and even sports, if you live in a certain kind of town. Don't talk about celebrities or other people in the news—like O.J. or Howard Stern or Tom Cruise or the pope—discussions of whom often reveal unattractive prejudices you or others might have. More often than not, people will surprise you with their point of view in these sorts of conversations and not in a good way. Don't you be the one surprising and shocking everyone else.

While you're at it, don't discuss salaries. Colleagues comparing pay stubs create the worst kind of headaches for their boss.

ASK YOURSELF:

► Have I ever gotten into an argument with a coworker over something that wasn't work related?

► Has anyone ever been offended by my language?

► Have I ever made a joke at someone else's expense?

► Has anyone at work ever called me a jerk?

► Is there anyone in my office whom I would consider loyal to me?

Even though salaries are the most interesting things to talk about at happy hour with your personal friends, they're poison to discuss at work. Don't bring them up, and don't let anyone draw you into a discussion about them. Period.

Keep your vocabulary G-rated. Wouldn't it be a crying shame to discover that while you've been enjoying your inalienable right to say any damn swearword you want to, your secretly devout supervisor has been making a mental note of your potty mouth? And given the choice to keep you or your upstanding, clean-living, hymn-humming cubemate when jobs are being cut, who do you think he'll pick? This also goes for talking about anything that might be the subject of a *Cosmo* self-test or appear on porn sites or that is generally discussed in the privacy of a gynecologist's office. Think about that stuff all day long if you want to, Joe Francis, just keep it to yourself.

Keep your hands to yourself, while you're at it. Even if you're one of those warm, cozy people who likes to punctuate conversation with a touch on the arm, it's better not to. People are sensitive and paranoid and litigious, and the last thing you want is for some innocent physical gesture to turn into grounds for some kind of harassment suit. No shoulder rubs, no hugs, nothing. Just don't touch.

P.S. Practical jokes and teasing are inappropriate, too. No one likes to be the butt of this kind of humor, and most people are uncomfortable even being around it. You don't win hearts by torturing your colleagues with even mildly cruel pranks. So leave the fake barf and whoopee cushion at home.

▶▶▶ *Behave yourself.*
▶▶▶ *Circumspection is a virtue in the workplace.*

19. DISCUSS, DON'T ARGUE

There's always some blowhard at work who turns every conversation into a battle. Don't be him. And don't argue with him, either.

A person who is automatically in an argue mode when interacting with coworkers is usually insecure, aggressive, or a volatile combination of both. Facts tend to be beside the point, and winning the argument is all that matters, regardless of the collateral damage. If your office climate is confrontational or competitive, it can add to this tendency, and you may even find yourself becoming contentious, even against your nature.

Discussions solve problems through consideration and deliberation. I'm not saying it's wrong to have a concrete opinion, because conviction is respectable, but the truth is that arguments tend to be vociferous discussions in which pointedly different opinions are aired for the purpose of self-justification rather than resolution. So to keep one from becoming the other, try to be the one to maintain control over a dialogue. Here's how:

- ▶ Be civil. Be deferential in your demeanor, use polite words, and avoid confrontational body language, such as pointing or folding your arms over your chest or banging your shoe on the table like Khrushchev.
- ▶ Be even. Control your temper and measure your tone of voice.
- ▶ Listen first. This is the most effective way to convince the other person that you respect his or her point of view.
- ▶ Be candid. Say your piece without mincing words. Be direct without being defensive.

TRUE STORY

I once worked with a big arguer, a real hothead named Tom. We had the same job, but he had more seniority and was a top performer with a giant ego. I mostly avoided mixing it up with this guy, but our company was going through a rough patch and I realized it might be a good time to distinguish myself from him as an employee. Knowing that the slightest thing would set him off, I'd provoke him just enough and then watch him show himself for the short fuse he had. People were on edge as it was, and no one liked listening to his abrasive contentiousness. And sure enough, before long, he was let go and my job was bulletproof. Sneaky? A little. But it's not as if I was giving him a problem he didn't already have.

▶ Acknowledge the disagreement. Restate the point of disagreement so you're both clear on it and so that you stick to the topic at hand and don't allow the conversation to degenerate into personal affronts.

▶ Identify areas of agreement, also known as "common ground." This is the path to resolution.

▶ Make a mutual plan to resolve the disagreement. Set aside the discussion to think about it and make a date to revisit. If you sort it out eventually, great. If not, be prepared to agree to disagree permanently.

All that said, sometimes arguments are unavoidable and you just have to process the issues and move on. Just don't become known as a chronic arguer. It makes you look as if you're angry and combative and don't care if you get along with others. If you take the high road and the strong, even hand in a discussion, you can keep it on track and productive for everyone involved. That's the sign of someone who'd rather keep his job than win every round.

▶▶▶ *Turn the impulse to argue into a resolution to resolve.*
▶▶▶ *Behave with civility when someone else initiates an argument.*

20. DON'T BE A GOSSIP

If this were another kind of book—or I were another kind of person—I'd tell you to avoid gossip altogether. If knowledge is power, then gossip is the neighborhood bully. It's the hoodlum waiting to jump you in a dark alley. It's fear-based and opportunistic, and it never has a good outcome. It generates hurtful misperceptions, confusion, pain, and conflict; it erodes trust and morale; and, finally, it wastes time.

Let's be real, though. Gossip is also tasty and titillating and irresistible. Being in the know—especially at work—gives us a buzz of superiority that's hard to beat. More to the point, much of the information that falls from the grapevine can be useful to you. Scuttlebutt about jobs, sales, mergers, and acquisitions usually has a grain of truth and should put you on orange alert. The bulletproof trick is to *have* the gossip but not to *be* the gossip. And what makes you be the gossip is not knowing it but repeating it.

The office gossip is admired and respected by no one—not your coworkers and not your boss. Every time you gossip, you send a message that you lack discretion and you simply can't be trusted—not the world's best way to hang on to your job.

And gossip is a two-way street. What you forget when you're

HOW TO GET OFF THE RUMOR MILL

Gossip is a vice like smoking and drinking that gives you a hangover when you've overindulged; after the exhilaration wears off, you feel sick to your stomach and regretful of all the bad will you've released into the atmosphere. If you just can't stand yourself anymore and you want to clean up your act, the tips below will take you through do-it-yourself gossip rehab.

▶ Commit to one hour a day when you will not share or listen to gossip. This will make you very conscious of the prevalence of gossip in your life and how easy it is to fall into if you're not paying attention. Increase to two hours, then three and so on, until your whole workday is a gossip-free zone.

▶ Before you repeat something you've heard, substitute your own name in place of the person the gossip is about. Would you be glad to hear this piece of information about yourself?

▶ Learn to excuse yourself when gossip is being shared. You don't have to be a sanctimonious prig about it; you can just smile, put your hands over your ears, say "TMI, TMI" and walk away. Just get yourself out of there.

▶ And when gossip inadvertently lands in your lap—you overhear it in the restroom or find something juicy left behind in the copier—do the right thing with it. If there are rumblings of mergers, personnel changes, or downsizing causing distress and decreased productivity, let your boss know about them. Management will be glad for the heads-up in order to quell unfounded rumors. If you hear gossip about a coworker you know isn't true, make him aware of the chatter to give him a fair chance to deal with it. And if you discover you're the subject of gossip, confront the source of the scoop directly. Gossips don't usually step in the same shit twice when they're called out on it.

THE SOUR GRAPEVINE

According to a 2007 Harris Interactive Poll, 60 percent of respondents describe gossip as the most distasteful aspect of their office culture. So why do we do it? *Psychology Today* calls gossip a "beehive of communication" humans rely on in order to network, influence others, and forge social alliances. Which is true only until our dark side takes over, at which point we find ourselves in a hornet's nest, where we gossip because we lack a healthy sense of self, we're insecure, and we're jealous of others. Apparently evolution doesn't make it any better. Because we're hardwired to survive and compete, we instinctively use language and our natural political radar to create advantage for ourselves at the expense of others.

on the dishing end is that being on the receiving end is just as dangerous. The minute you give up the goods on someone else, a target appears on your own back. That's not very smart either.

So don't *be* the office gossip; *be friends* with the office gossip. That's because, as noted above, knowledge is power and the information you gather from gossip can provide the extra bit of power you need to stay ahead of the game. The trick is to absorb the information without repeating it, to appear to be above it even while you're filing it away for future reference to use, if necessary, to bulletproof your job. Example: A friend happened to hear a rumor of his company being acquired, and he asked me what to do about it. I told him, whatever you do, don't go on vacation. If something happens, you have to be there to defend your job. As expected, the rumor turned out to be truth, and he was ready and able to bulletproof his job.

No one is immune to gossip, but knowing the gossip can protect you from being the victim of it.

Bosses pretend they hate gossip, but in reality they love it. Or, at least, they *rely* on it. Most good bosses and many top CEOs manage their own power with the help of gossip. Everyone knows it, but no one says that company morale is measured by sticking a thermometer up the ass of the office gossip. So it's important to the boss in order to monitor the mood and culture of the company. Let me be clear, though. Do *not* be the person who gets the thermometer up the ass—but know who that person is. Be close to that person privately, but publicly, well, pretend you don't know him or her.

So when you find yourself in possession of a sizzling hot piece of information about someone, something you're *dying* to share with one coworker about another, don't. Put it in the vault. File it away. Refuse to engage. Just say no.

▶▶▶ **Listen to gossip but never repeat it.**
▶▶▶ **Use what you learn through gossip very carefully.**

21. UNDERSTAND YOUR OFFICE POLITICS

Any company that claims it has no office politics is lying to itself, and only stupid employees believe it. Every workplace has politics, and it's important to know yours—and to remember that politics are constantly changing. Politics exist on the assembly line, in the retail store, at the hospital, and at the high school. And there's no such thing as being "above" office politics. Whether you're actively engaged in them or not, you're threatened by them, even more so when jobs are being cut. People who say they're "above" office politics are like people who tell me they refuse to own a cell phone. It's cheap moral superiority.

That said, like gossip, politics are everywhere, and in the same way you don't want to be known for being the office gossip, you don't want to be known for being a political operator either. Trying to ignore the political shenanigans isn't a very clever bulletproof strategy. Office politics are the expression of ambition and the competition to get ahead that are a natural part of the culture of work. But employees who spend more time stirring up the political dust—sabotaging people they don't like or undercutting those who get in their way—than doing their jobs well are rarely considered worth the trouble when push comes to shove.

In addition, unless you're really, really good at office politics, you should never try to play them. Ordinary people aren't the Machiavellian masters they need to be for playing politics to work in their favor. So while you don't want to draw attention to yourself as someone in the thick of all the power plays and petty maneuvering, you do want to be aware of what's going on and be prepared to fall into the slipstream of circumstances that might work to your advantage. Think of yourself as an active spectator—tuned in to the action, astute about your own behavior, but otherwise minding your own business. The best way to fly under the radar is to make a point of knowing what's going on without letting people know you know.

The political dynamic of each office is different; it depends on the personalities and personal and professional agendas of you, your coworkers, your managers, and all the way up to the CEO. It can play out like a bitterly fought war (Hewlett-Packard, anyone?) or a friendly game of poker. Either way, your concern should be to know which way the wind is blowing and to stay out of the political cross fire. Here's how:

▶ Be honest and open about your own agenda. You have a goal, but don't be so subtle about it that people scrutinize your intentions. You don't want colleagues—or worse, your boss—to begin to wonder if you're after their jobs. Whatever the case, don't be a sneak.

▶ Do not ally yourself with one faction or another. Listen to all sides and form your own opinions, but don't publicly take sides.

▶ Do not be drawn into anyone's attempts to win you over against another. Put up a neutral front at all times. To your colleagues, you're Switzerland.

▶ Don't go over people's heads. This always stinks of political maneuvering and puts you in a nasty light when you get caught doing it.

All this will help you in two ways. When things go wrong, as they are wont to do in the office O.K. Corral, you're not likely to be rounded up with the bad guys and punished by association. At the same time, you're in a decent position to let the good political outcomes of others spill over a bit onto your own situation. In this case, proximity is everything, so if you're not paying attention and miss the whole shoot-out, well, just be glad you weren't injured. But if you're on your toes, you may just benefit from shifting political tides, including possible regime change. When someone moves on as a result of political fallout, for example, you can already have floated your availability for and interest in the job. Slick!

▶ ▶ ▶   *Be aware of the politics going on in your office, but don't become a player.*

▶ ▶ ▶   *Understand the intraoffice alliances and divisions among your bosses and colleagues, but avoid taking sides.*

22. BE POSITIVE

There are all kinds of reasons to choose to be a positive person over being a negative person, not least because it usually makes your own life much more pleasant. But let's skip ahead to what makes it such an important part of your strategy for bulletproofing your job. In short, positive people are easy to work with and negative people are not. And *smart* positive people are among the most valuable in the workplace. Keepers, if you will.

You know the naturally positive people—the smiley-face folks, the ones who always think the cup's half full—especially in contrast to the negative folks, the Eeyores, the pessimists, the ones who don't even need to look at the cup to tell you it's empty, man.

So what exactly is a positive attitude? It's a combination of an appropriate expression of emotion (smiles and other affirming body language versus frowns, snarls, and visible disgust, for example); a sustained expression of mood that is cheerful and constructive versus sour and destructive; and your general disposition, which features an optimistic and hopeful view of outcomes versus a gloomy or cynical expectation. Given the choice, whom do you think your coworkers would rather be around? How about your boss? And what about your clients or customers? That's why being positive is bulletproof gold.

There's good news: unlike your height or your crazy fam-

THE POWER OF BEING POSITIVE

A positive person thinks in these terms: I can, I am able, I will. And generally, that kind of thinking gets results. A positive person is *always* more productive than a negative person, and don't think your boss won't notice that.

Positivity has a striking influence on others. It boosts group morale, strengthens the team, and improves productivity, which in turn reduces turnover, chronic absenteeism, and general slackerism. When *you're* considered the source of this kind of influence, not only are you bulletproof, you're considered leadership material. Hello, promotion!

Positivity drives change. Or at least it paves the way for change, which most people resist fiercely when left to their own devices. The enthusiasm, collaboration, and mutual support that result from even a single person's positive influence in the workplace can be the difference between a culture of employees who willingly contribute to necessary change and those who fight and sabotage change, which in turn can be the difference between a company that succeeds or fails in a difficult climate. If your company continues to do well in spite of a tough economy, guess who will come out looking like a superhero?

Even a powerful negative person will eventually be overcome by the force of positivity. This doesn't mean you can "save" him and he'll miraculously become the positive, supportive boss you've always dreamed of; it just means you can neutralize some or all of his negative impact just by keeping positive pressure on your interactions and communication with him and others. This is good for you, good for the company, and, whether he likes it or not, it's good for him, too.

ily, you have significant control over your attitude. You can choose to be positive—and to set off the whole chain of positive influence—simply by identifying your current worldview and habits and making conscious positive adjustments. Or you can

TRUE STORY

Bobbie, a graphic designer for a large agency, was told in a performance review that she had such a negative attitude that some people were refusing to work with her. She was shocked by this, having no idea that she was perceived this way and suddenly gravely worried for her job security. Motivated to turn the situation around, she asked a longtime associate for his honest assessment of her attitude as well as some specifics about her behavior that might help her make some changes. The feedback he shared that made the biggest impression? "You sit in brainstorming meetings with your lips pursed and your arms folded over your chest, and all you ever offer are the reasons someone's ideas aren't going to work."

So Bobbie created a simple plan to modify her behavior, starting with her body language. At the next staff meeting to discuss a new product campaign, she made a point of sitting with her limbs uncrossed and with a pointedly relaxed and pleasant face. And instead of criticizing her associates, she began posing simple, productive questions and suggestions (instead of playing her usual "devil's advocate") that helped the team improve on its ideas. Bobbie worked at making a habit of this behavior, and soon her colleagues were coming to her for advice and feedback about their work. She went from being a dreaded plague to being a welcome and valued influence in a matter of months. Her bonus triumph in turning herself from Negative Nellie into Positive Polly? When she cured herself of the loud sighing that she discovered her coworkers had been making fun of behind her back for years.

skip all that (which I'm inclined to do—it could take a lifetime to turn that ship around!) and perfect the art of *acting* positive.

All you have to do is *smile*. Many managers have told me they have fired certain employees because they never smiled. Apparently bosses take smiles very personally. So if you have half a brain you'll smile all the time, whether you feel like it or not. That's right, fake it. ☺

Are you a furrowed-brow scowler? Practice face relaxation techniques and make a point of smiling at every person you speak to. Do you show up at work every day with a blue hangover from the breakup you're still getting over? Visualize that you're turning a page and stepping into a bright, hopeful future every time you walk through the door at work. If all that's too much, just fake a smile. Either approach will work. And try to expect the most positive outcome possible for every short—and long-term task. Or else, of course, just smile.

▶▶▶ *Demonstrate a positive attitude in your work and relationships.*

▶▶▶ *Smile, smile, smile.*

ASK YOURSELF:

▶ Do I generally expect positive outcomes?

▶ Do I give myself credit for my accomplishments?

▶ Do I generally think the best of someone else's intentions?

▶ Do I usually compliment others when things turn out well?

▶ Do others come to me for encouragement or positive reinforcement?

23. BE DEPENDABLE

This one is easy: Do what you say you're going to do. Every single time.

If you tell someone you're going to have a report ready by 3:00, turn it in at 2:55, then give yourself five minutes to sneak a smoke in the bathroom. Just kidding about the smoke. But not kidding about turning it in on time, every time.

Being dependable is at the heart of trust, a crucial commodity in the workplace. Your boss and your coworkers need to know they can absolutely, positively count on you to deliver on your promises to them. It takes time—and many instances of your doing exactly what you say you'll do—to build that trust, but you need to drop the ball only once to set the dependability meter back to zero. In one disappointing instant, you transform yourself from an indispensable resource to an unreliable flake. So don't say you'll do something, be somewhere, or say something if you can't pull it off. There is simply too much at stake—your job.

This does not mean you should avoid promising anything at all so that you never have to break a promise. That would make you someone with commitment issues, my friend, and while your long-suffering boyfriend or girlfriend may let you get away with it, your boss and colleagues won't.

Being dependable is about getting to work on time, not missing work for lame reasons, not missing meetings or deadlines, and giving people what they ask for in a timely fashion. When people know they can count on you to meet these basic obligations, they will entrust you with more responsibility and your stock within the organization will rise.

But true dependability is a sign of total commitment. It's all

JUST SO YOU KNOW

Being a glad-handing yes-man doesn't make you dependable. Some people have a sad tendency to say yes to everyone so that people will like them. Unfortunately, this sets them up to disappoint everyone, too. Better to say to someone, "Gee, I'd like to help you with your project, but I won't be able to get to it today," than to say "Sure!" and then not help him, leaving him holding the bag in one hand and a sharp ax to grind against you in the other. You owe it to your boss and colleagues to be honest about what you can and can't do. And if you can't do it too much of the time, guess what? Either you're not working hard enough or you're in way over your head. Either way, you're probably in trouble. Being realistic with yourself and others about what you can accomplish is as important as the follow-through.

or nothing, so being 99 percent dependable isn't enough. When you're undependable, people avoid working with you because you put their own success at risk. Instead they'll gravitate toward others they can count on—and gripe to the boss about how unreliable *you* are, in which case you can pretty much count the days until you'll be looking for a new job.

Other than tragic personal loss, there's no excuse for missing a deadline or blowing a delivery. And offering excuses suggests buck-passing of the worst kind. There's no such thing as extenuating circumstances.

▶▶▶ *Be sure your colleagues and your boss know they can rely on you.*

▶▶▶ *Make dependability a defining trait.*

24. BE FLEXIBLE

Most of us would like our work environment to be more flexible to accommodate our interests and obligations outside work. Well, I've got news for you: if you're even remotely concerned about your job security, you need to be thinking about how you can make life easier for your employer by being flexible, not the other way around. I know, I know, Norma Rae is going to hunt me down like a dog for talking like that. But the fact is, being a flexible, adaptable employee instead of a rigid, demanding employee when the going is rough can *save your job.*

Flexible employees—the ones who keep a good attitude during change, who go with the flow instead of fighting it, who cheerfully offer to fill in gaps and pitch in as needed—these are the folks who tend to survive a layoff.

Being flexible is simple. It means being nice, going the extra mile, and being cooperative. Being flexible isn't about being a weenie, it's about being agreeable and versatile and valuable. It's about being an active part of solutions to problems. It's about not digging in your heels when what your boss needs most is for you to be loose and open to switching gears. Remember: your boss, like the customer, is always right. Does this make you a doormat? Maybe. The fact is, doormats almost always keep their jobs.

Be prepared for change. In a volatile economy or an emerging industry, change is the norm. So be ready for it. Approach your work with an understanding and acceptance of the necessity of change, and you'll develop the sea legs that allow you to thrive in those conditions. Being adaptable to change isn't just a state of mind; it's a skill your employer will value dearly. So instead of stiffening up and resisting a new, difficult, or disagreeable sce-

TRUE STORY

Jim worked in the marketing department of an online pet supply company that was hot, hot, hot before the dot-com bubble burst and then hung on by its fingernails for several years after that. As employees were cut in waves of layoffs all around him, Jim leaned into the new challenges every day brought, keeping up a can-do attitude even as he was being asked to take on more responsibilities, including many he'd never had before. One day he'd be working on marketing materials. The next, he'd be accompanying his boss on sales calls. The day after that, he'd be helping the fulfillment guys do warehouse inventory. When the company finally righted itself, just barely avoiding insolvency, Jim was one of the last of the front-office employees standing. By rising to the occasion and rolling with a difficult situation that changed daily, he ended up not just with his job but with an emotional and financial stake in the company he helped keep afloat.

nario, let go of your preconceived notions and just see where the situation takes you. Keep an open mind.

Think of your work experience as a journey on which you may take some interesting alternative routes. Say you're a sales manager at a retail company and your boss asks you to help develop the seasonal catalog for the company. Hey, I've never done that before! I don't know how! It's not my job! Quit crying and just do it. (A) It shows you're flexible, and (B) it shows you're game to learn.

Be flexible because you'll create new opportunities for yourself. And because there may not be a more valuable attribute than flexibility when flux rules the day.

▶▶▶ *Show that you're open to change.*
▶▶▶ *Prove that you're valuable during changing times.*

25. ENCOURAGE OTHERS

There was a time when your mom and your soccer coach and your best friend and your boss knew just how to offer the perfect word of encouragement that would help you feel good about yourself and make you want to keep going, improve yourself, and accomplish great things. No more.

Now people pay cash money to "life coaches" to tell them they're doing a good job and help them organize their closets. Beyond that, it's every man for himself. This could be why the self-help book industry is continually thriving (but that's another matter).

The fact is, encouraging others is easy. It's a simple pat on the back, a show of goodwill that costs nothing to the person who gives it and benefits the recipient immeasurably. A recent study showed that praise gives most people as big a psychological boost as money does. So when a peer or a subordinate or even your boss is doing a good job, tell them. It's an old-school attribute that could make you a new-school hero at work. Here's how.

JUST SO YOU KNOW

Here's my secret weapon: Tell people they're doing a good job *even when they're not.* Or perhaps I should say *especially* when they're not. They get a nice boost, and you continue to charge ahead in the contest between you and your coworkers to keep your jobs. Play nice, but be smart about it.

There's a wonderful ripple effect when you encourage others. Recognizing someone else's work or accomplishment sets off a chain reaction of positive reinforcement. Feeling appreciated increases his sense of well-being, which he then passes on to others. The beauty of this is that it works on anyone—your assistant, your associate, your boss, even the CEO. I have a friend who once walked up to Yankees baseball star Bernie Williams early in his career and said, "You're doing a great job, and I think you're going to be a Yankee legend." Though you'd hardly imagine *he'd* need a pat on the back, he said, "Thank you, that means a lot to me," humbled and visibly touched by her praise. The point is, *everybody* needs encouragement.

Encouraging others requires only a simple shift in the way you operate from day to day. All you have to do is pay attention. That's it. Quit thinking about yourself for a change, and show an interest in the people you work with. Acknowledge their good efforts. When someone does a great job in a presentation or beats his sales goals or writes a great report, say so. And if you can, share your praise in front of the group, or send an e-mail to him and copy his bosses or colleagues. This multiplies the value of the encouragement to the recipient and shows you to be a positive, supportive, encouraging influence on others.

For some people the occasional "Atta boy" and "Well done" can make the difference between giving up and sticking to it. So don't be stingy with your compliments. Show an interest by asking questions. Take it a step further and ask for advice. "Can you show me how you dropped that video into your PowerPoint?" Nothing is more flattering or validating than treating someone else like an expert.

When you introduce someone, brag about him a little. "This is Bill, he's that tech genius on our team I've been telling you

ASK YOURSELF:

► Do people think of me as someone who encourages others, pays no attention to them, or brings them down?

► When was the last time I complimented someone at work (and *not* about those kick-ass new Sigerson Morrison boots)?

► Have I ever observed someone in need of encouragement? Did I offer it?

► Have I ever surprised someone with a compliment?

► What kind of encouragement from someone else gives *me* a lift?

about." And if it's appropriate to the situation, share your praise of someone's work with his boss.

Find a way to offer appreciation, recognition, and encouragement whenever you can. Acknowledgement of the good efforts of others creates goodwill and positive energy and strengthens the group. It also makes you look like a team player *and* a leader, a golden asset in any job climate.

►►► *Be generous with praise.*

26. SHARE CREDIT

The best way to get all the credit you think you deserve for your accomplishments on the job is to give it away. This might seem a little risky when the job economy is iffy or change is in the air. You may feel tempted to toot your own horn more than usual out of fear of your good work not being noticed or valued. It is, in fact, even more important to share credit with colleagues during difficult times. That's because it shows management that you have class, that you're playing for the team, and that you're not just out for yourself.

Even if you're the one who's primarily responsible for the success of a project, by taking the lead in crediting your coworkers for their efforts or support, you receive all the benefits of the success of your work, plus a little bit extra in the eyes of your employers for showing modesty and generosity. Sharing the glory for a job well done—instead of splitting hairs over who did what—generates a lot of goodwill and group esteem. An added bonus is that your coworkers will be motivated to work with you

SMART WAYS TO SPREAD CREDIT AROUND

▶ Say it in person—a sincere thank-you to every colleague who contributed to a successful effort is always welcome and remembered.

▶ Say it in public—giving props to your team at the appropriate company meeting gives a good impression of them and of you.

▶ Say it in writing—if the situation allows, circulate a memo recognizing your team's accomplishment. Tout sales, schedule, or budget milestones to your boss on behalf of the team. Send around an e-mail about the above-and-beyond efforts of a certain person or two.

▶ Say it to yourself—and mean it. If you don't genuinely believe your colleagues deserve to share credit with you, no one's going to believe you when you say they do. You can't pretend to be generous with credit.

JUST SO YOU KNOW

The opposite of sharing credit is sharing blame. While you should share credit at any opportunity, you should share blame very rarely. Take responsibility for your own mistakes, and speak generally for the group—as necessary—when problems occur. But never single out another person for blame in public or in private. And if you're put on the spot by your boss for an accounting of who did what when things went wrong, tread carefully. Be moderate and matter-of-fact in your tone and only as specific as is absolutely necessary. Vaguely defend the party in question and then shut up. Blamers are held in the same low regard as credit grabbers.

again because you recognized the value of their contribution and publicly shared credit with them.

When you take it on yourself to publicize your accomplishment on behalf of the group, you convey your primary ownership of that accomplishment without seeming as if you're grandstanding. No one likes a credit hog—even if he deserves the lion's share of the credit.

Sharing credit is one of the few things I advocate simply because it's the right thing to do. It's smart and classy and always, always pays off.

▶▶▶ *Cultivate a reputation for sharing credit.*
▶▶▶ *Be sincere when offering credit.*

27. STAY CALM

Check out the want ads. Jobs ranging from customer service reps to RNs to tax accountants to tech analysts to risk management specialists to manicurists call for the candidates to have the ability to stay calm and professional during busy, stressful, or emergency situations. These job descriptions ask for a "calm personality"; the ability to stay "calm, cool, and collected" during a crisis; to "handle stressful situations in a calm, professional manner"; to offer a "calm, reassuring response" to clients or customers who are feeling stressed or agitated; and to be able to communicate in a "clear, calm manner."

Why is this such a valuable skill? Because in many cases, people freak out under pressure and cause an already difficult crisis to get worse because they couldn't keep their heads on straight. This also tends to cause a mob response, a kind of running for the exits when someone yells "Fire!" in a movie theater. Lovely.

Staying calm is just what the term implies. Let's just say you can demonstrate that ability when your boss and coworkers need it most. Example: You discover that someone on your team has totally dropped the ball on his part of a report your boss is supposed to be presenting tomorrow. You calmly get to work on the report, knowing you'll probably be at it all night. Meanwhile, the guy in the cube next to you runs around like a ninny, panicking and hyperventilating and making the already stressed climate worse with his histrionics. Hmmm. Which of you do you think will get the pass on the pink slip?

Some people are naturally calm. The rest of us can teach ourselves how to *seem* calm, which is all that really matters anyway. So what if there's a tornado of anxiety swirling inside you as long as you present a calm façade? If you have the opportunity to

turn a situation in which everyone else is frantic into an opportunity for you to look like a cool, collected life raft, take it.
Here's how:

▶ Identify the source of the stress. Did your team just lose its
biggest account? Did someone blow a big presentation? Have
you all just heard the rumor about a reorganization in your division? Decide how much control you have over what has happened or what might happen. Ninety-nine percent of the time
you'll realize you have no immediate control over the outcome
of situations like these, so take a moment to recognize that in order to put a little distance between yourself and the source of
stress.

▶ Create a response ritual. When the stress-o-meter is clang-
ing like crazy all around you, revert to a calming habit that helps
you keep your bearings. First, breathe. Inhale slowly through
your nose, then exhale slowly through your mouth. Repeat until
your breathing is the boss of you. This will help you shake off the
paralysis that a real doozy of a crisis can bring on. Leave the
room, take a short walk, give yourself a minute to collect your
thoughts.

▶ *Now* you can think about what you can do be a part of the
solution to the stressful situation. Your boss will be grateful if
you simply don't contribute to the existing chaos. And if you can
think on your feet in a crisis—you know, like one of those people
in a disaster movie who stays calm enough to make the plan to
lead others to safety—your boss might credit you with saving his
job, too.

Part of staying calm, for yourself and others, is to be in possession of the facts when people are being upset by rumors or

misinformation, which is often the case during a crisis. If you can't get your hands on the facts, don't make the situation worse by perpetuating rumors.

Hear the voice of a nightly news anchor in your head. These people have their jobs more for their calming demeanor than their journalistic prowess. Keep your own voice even and low, and the people around you will follow suit. Staying focused on a task at hand will also have a calming effect on others. Most of the other "be easy" rules can help you be the commandant of calm in a pinch as well: Don't get drawn into arguments (number 19), avoid gossip (number 20) and finger-pointing, be positive (number 22), be flexible (number 24). When you and your co-workers come out of the other end of a difficult situation, they'll remember who kept the ship from capsizing. *You.*

Finally, try to look calm. If you're neurotic or nervous or unsure or a downright wreck, don't show it. You can't change who you are, but you can change the way you behave and how you are perceived. Ducks are calm on the surface but paddle like mad below the surface where you can't see. Be a duck.

▶▶▶ *Resist the urge to panic.*
▶▶▶ *Present a calm demeanor.*
▶▶▶ *Show that you can help solve problems during crisis.*

BULLETPROOF TAKEAWAY

I won't kid you about this. If you've been a royal pain all your life, becoming easy won't be easy. There's a lot of basic stuff about your difficult personality that there isn't enough time in the world to change. But you—and the less obstinate among you—can set yourself on a path of amateur behavior modification right now that might not change you but can surely change what happens to you when your job is on the line.

▶ Quit complaining about, ragging on, and tussling with your coworkers, bringing your personal problems to work, and otherwise misbehaving.

▶ Stay out of the fray of office gossip and politics.

▶ Buff up your easygoing image by behaving in a positive and flexible way, encouraging and sharing credit with others, and staying calm in a crisis.

In short, do everything you must to avoid being known as a high-maintenance employee.

3

BE USEFUL

In bulletproof times, even an idiot knows to put his head down and *act* as if he's working. But acting will get you only so far; you need to be useful. Luckily, being useful is mostly just doing the job your employer is paying you to do. Except, you know, actually *doing* it. And all that stuff you've been slacking off on or avoiding or pawning off on other people, such as giving your boss bad news or calling a client about an outstanding invoice? Well, now you have to do that, too. And finally, you have to actively look for ways to do more.

That's right. It's time to become Mr. or Ms. Above and Beyond. The one who knows how to balance what you're paid to do with a strategic handful of "stretch" efforts—better known as extra credit—that give the clear impression of your invaluable utility. Of course, everything you're doing is useful and beneficial to the company and will earn you wings and half a halo. But it's the "more" that will set you apart from your slothful colleagues. And I don't mean that you should work more hours—or even that

you should work more. I mean you should d**o more to show how
damn useful you are.**

28. BE A MENTOR

One of the biggest drags on a company is high turnover at the junior levels. When a company makes an entry-level or junior hire,
it makes an investment in training and acclimating that is meant
to give the employee the skills to do his new job and the support
he needs to grow and advance, which, ideally, will develop into
loyalty and commitment to the company. Unfortunately, most
companies offer job training but not the ongoing support to
make a new employee feel like a permanent fixture in the company family. In a perfect world, the new employee's supervisor
and immediate coworkers would bring him along. In reality, this
kind of support exists only occasionally in the modern workplace
and is rarely institutionalized. Here's where you come in.

Beyond the expense of recruiting, interviewing, reference
checking, drug testing, benefit registration, and setting him up
with pencils and Post-its, it costs your company a lot of dough
every time it trains an employee only to see him leave soon after
he starts. And make no mistake about it, it costs you and your
coworkers, too, as you have to pick up the slack every time one
of these prospects doesn't work out. So how about if you step up
and offer a bit of support that will help these newbies feel a connection that will make them want to stay in the game and get
with the program—oh, and maybe give you a hand with all that
paperwork piling up on your desk.

Let's be clear: mentoring is for *you*, not for your mentee. It allows you to plant seeds of influence and support throughout

REVERSE MENTORING

Even very junior employees can play mentor—in reverse—by sharing knowledge that is unique to their age group and experience. Teaching older employees shortcuts on their computers or how to navigate social networking sites is a way to showcase your distinctive skills, turning you from an employee into an expert—click!—just like that. If you notice someone struggling, say, with a new program, offer to help. The answer will almost always be "Yes, thanks!" And now you have a higher-up in your debt.

your company and your industry that will grow and become more valuable to you over time. You don't have to have a staff or be a manager to be in the position to be a mentor. You just need to know the ropes of your workplace and have some experience that would be helpful to someone else. The most junior staff and recent hires are generally the most in need of this kind of support; all you have to do is offer.

Say you see a new kid struggling with an office system or nervous about interacting with a grumpy supervisor. At the right private moment, introduce yourself and offer a sympathetic word. Let him know that you understand how he feels and you can probably give him some tips to get past the learning curve on his new job. Simply say, "Drop me an e-mail sometime and let's have lunch." If he needs the guidance as much as you suspect, he'll seek you out. Then, if he seems smart, likable, and eager to succeed, offer to be a mentor.

In the same variety of ways your mentors have helped you, you may very well end up being a teacher, a resource, a sympathetic ear, and an ally to your mentee, depending on his needs and how well you get along. You'll be a valuable reality check, a critical source of advice and feedback, and a guide to the occasionally bumpy roads at work that you've already traveled. In turn, your mentees will become your little "sleeper cell" of support and intelligence seeded throughout the company and beyond, as they build their careers in the years to come.

Here are some simple guidelines for putting yourself to good and valuable use as a mentor:

▶ Keep things informal. This isn't the military. There doesn't need to be a rigid protocol or rules or schedules. You do need to make it clear how you would like the relationship to work. If you would prefer to speak in person rather than exchanging e-mails, for example, regarding issues you're discussing, say that. He's new, you're a veteran. You tell him how things will work best, and he'll follow your lead.

▶ Meet regularly. It doesn't matter if you prefer to meet once a week for breakfast or catch up once a month after work. Just be sure that you establish a regular pattern of communication she can count on. And know that it won't go on forever. Like good therapy, it does end eventually, usually when she gets her first promotion or when she's good enough at her job that she's giving *you* pointers. Beyond that, make it clear that you'll always be available in a crisis.

▶ Keep it professional. It may be very tempting to go out to Thursday happy hours with your mentee and his college buddies. I mean, they're fun! They're funny! It's Two-for-One Night! Resist the urge and maintain the distance and decorum that will allow your relationship to work for both of you. Your mentee is looking to you as the authority who sets and sticks to the boundaries you establish.

▶ Keep up the connection. Being an ally goes both ways. Once you've finished turning another employee from a greenie into a crackerjack up-and-comer, he becomes as valuable to your network as you are to his. He will go on to other jobs, but he will always remember the role you played in launching him in the work world. So will the many others that you may end up mentoring over ten years or so. Think how valuable that will be when *they've* become the Big Bosses!

▶▶▶ *Mentor new or younger employees to grow your sleeper cell of supporters.*

29. TRAIN OTHERS

Here's a secret for you: bosses hate to train people. Training is a pain and a bore, and bosses are lazy about it. So if you can train a new employee—or an existing employee—in an area in which you have a particular skill—in other words, do your boss's job for free—you're golden. This is especially true in a small company that doesn't have a formal training department and most bosses have to train employees themselves. It's a win-win for both your boss and you. When you do it well, your boss sees that you're looking out for his interests. And your trainee respects and appreciates your help, becoming another member of your sleeper cell of support in the organization.

Training a new employee takes patience. Every job should have a handbook written by an existing employee that describes tasks and responsibilities associated with the job. Special instructions should be noted, as well as recurring challenges that can be expected. If this handbook doesn't exist, you might have to write it. Inform your boss that you'd like to do this, and he's likely to encourage the undertaking. Then enlist appropriate employees to write their job descriptions, and now you have your employee instruction manual. If the booklet is useful and firmly in keeping with company protocol, the fact that you assembled this company bible will be remembered.

Rome wasn't built in a day, and job training doesn't happen like that either. Information associated with training can be overwhelming, so sharing it gradually and in stages can be effective. Give the new employee time to learn, make mistakes, ask questions. Make sure he or she knows you're open and available to answer questions for as long as it takes. (As long as it takes doesn't mean forever, though. If someone isn't "getting" his or her job after three months, you have to give your boss a heads-up.) Provide regular progress reports to your boss—because he needs them, of course, but also so you get full credit for what you're doing. Training a new employee is a lifesaver for your boss; just be smart enough to be sure you're not training your replacement!

The other opportunity you have to train other people is that of existing employees who could use some strengthening in the areas you've already mastered. Let's say you write the best project proposals on the planet. You know it, your boss knows it, your coworkers know it. What if you told your boss that you'd be willing to offer a little tutorial on your tricks and tips for writing a killer proposal? It'd take an hour, you could do it in the conference room, and it would be for anyone who wants to attend. How generous, your boss thinks. And how helpful that would be to everyone else, the ones who write all those lame proposals he has to spend so much time doctoring up. "Sure, that would be great, thanks!" he says.

Now who's the bigger winner here—you, your boss, or your

coworkers? You look like a hero, your boss is probably going to start to see some improved product, and your coworkers may well improve their own standing by making an effort to be better at their jobs. Let's just call it a draw.

Find the right way to share your special skill, technique, or practical insight. Offering it one-on-one to people you think might need it is fine, but make sure your boss is aware of your efforts. If it's appropriate to offer to train people as a group, as in the example above, do that, too. Perhaps you can make yourself available regularly to train new employees in a particular system in which you're known to be proficient. That would become an ongoing opportunity to flaunt your expertise and add value at the same time.

But while you're trying to increase your own stock by highlighting your talent, you need to share your specialty in a way that doesn't make your colleagues want to sock you. What? They won't just hug you and thank you and bring you gifts of frankincense and myrrh? No, not if you're acting like a know-it-all snick. Be humble and gracious and forgiving of their lack of skill. Be sincere and supportive and show them that you're doing it to benefit the whole company. Because if they smell that you're a self-serving opportunist, they *will* sock you.

Share your enthusiasm for your area of specialty. This is the best way to motivate others to improve their own skills—to get them to do so because they want to, not because they *have* to. Say you're the finest blacksmith in the county and everyone within a hundred miles comes to you to have their horses shod. Sharing your passion for your own excellent work with your trainees is the quickest way to turn them into a little bunch of skilled experts. And then you have a valuable team and a new batch of loyal recruits.

Are you starting to see the pattern emerging here? You share, it makes you look good, it makes your boss look good, it helps other people, and it makes *them* look good, too. I'm the last person to preach altruism, but if it helps me bulletproof my job, sign me up!

▶▶▶ *Offer to train coworkers to save your boss from doing it.*
▶▶▶ *Share your skills to show off your skills.*

30. BE A UTILITY PLAYER

Here's a multiple-choice question for you: The woman in the cube next to you has taken a job with your company's biggest competitor and left your boss holding the bag on a big presentation coming up next week. Do you:

A. Shrink down in your chair and hope your boss doesn't call on you to fill in. You can't remember the last time you made a presentation!

B. Tell him you'd like to help but it's "not your job."

C. Hop off the bench and get yourself up to speed on the project as quick as you can.

Pens down. By now you know that the bulletproof answer is *always* C. The formula is simple: Suck up, do the work, and go a step farther than everyone else. This is one of those golden opportunities to be truly indispensable, roll up your sleeves, use your whole range of skills, and help pull the rabbit out the hat. Seriously.

When you're trying to establish your long-term value, you have to cultivate the perception that you have superior skills in a

TRUE STORY

Richard was his team's top account exec and had been for a long time. One weekend, his division was preparing a huge client pitch on which he'd been the lead writer; Richard's work on the project had been done for weeks, and the presentation was now in the hands of the art department. He was about to head out for a Saturday afternoon of golf when he got a frantic call from the design assistant telling him the art director had gone into labor and she wasn't sure she could pull the project together herself. He was the only one she could think of who might be able to help. Actually, his was the only name she could think of at all.

Richard was no art director, but he knew the project well enough that he could probably help the poor kid pull it off. With the help of one intern and the design assistant's mother, they finished correcting, printing, and binding the last of the proposal materials on Sunday night, to be shipped for the Tuesday presentation. In eighteen hours, Richard proofread the entire proposal, tweaked countless lines of copy, did a bunch of Quark-XPress monkey work he used to know how to do, supervised the printing of about a million photocopies, and assembled, packed, and addressed a dozen cartons for UPS pickup. Sure, he could have called in the cavalry, but it felt good to flex some work muscles he hadn't used in a while. And it looked pretty good, too.

particular area at the same time that you have a broad skill set that can save the day in a pinch. Just doing your own job well isn't enough; you should be prepared to hustle when you have to and do the next guy's job and some other guy's, too. Being a utility player requires that you be ready (that is, prepared and willing) and able (which is to say, you have a broad enough skill set that you can play several roles).

In sports, a utility player is someone who's generally capable of filling in at a number of positions. He's a jack-of-all-trades, though usually a master of none. I'm advising you, however, to be the master of your primary position *and* to be adept at a handful of others so that you have a skill set that can be counted on in any number of ways when your boss needs it most. Think of someone like Magic Johnson, who was the best point guard in basketball—famous for pulling off some amazing behind-the-back passes—but who was prepared to post up against a seven-foot center in a pinch if the situation called for it.

To become that most-appreciated utility player, you can draw on skills you used earlier in your career or some skills you have yet to acquire but are interested in learning. You just need to be willing to stretch and volunteer and be ready to be called off the bench in an emergency. Be aware that your boss may not know any more than you do about how to deal with a situation, so don't be afraid to wing it. There will likely be a steep learning curve. And you'll get bonus points for your fearlessness.

Be grateful for the chance to jump in when it happens. Because if your boss knows you are multifaceted, adaptable, and willing to pitch in, um, you'll keep your job. Trust me.

▶ ▶ ▶ *Demonstrate a variety of skills that can make you useful in a variety of ways.*

31. BE A SPECIALIST

Okay, now that I've convinced you to be an all-around generalist, I'm telling you that you have to be a specialist, too. That's because although people appreciate the broad skill set you've amassed that can be exploited in a variety of ways, they will value you even more if you are a sharpshooter—a uniquely skilled razzle-dazzle artist they can count on to do something no one else can.

You don't go to your GP for brain surgery, you go to the guy with all the letters after his name and the Ivy League diplomas on his wall indicating he has all the superspecial, ultraprecise training that's going to save your life. That's who *you* want to be: the brain surgeon.

So how can you go about developing a specialty? Within a general area of responsibility, there are any number of tasks you can turn into a forte. Say you're a book editor with a passion for knitting. Focus on this area of interest and become known for the beautiful craft books you publish. If you work the sales floor of a hardware store and you have a flair for grilling, make sure no

TRUE STORY

Vin was a mechanical designer for a big consumer products company. He'd been there for nearly twenty years, much longer than many of his slick young coworkers. That was because he had always made a point of being the earliest adopter of new technology, moving swiftly from the hand drawings he created early in his career to 2-D computer-aided design programs and to mastery of the 3-D programs his coworkers were slow or reluctant to learn. He regularly took advanced design courses and consciously, constantly improved and honed his skills, making himself the in-house expert to be consulted on cutting-edge technology. And when job cuts came, as they would from time to time, Vin always had a necessary expertise, and he stayed on while others, well, didn't.

one knows more about the barbecues and grill equipment than you do. Take an avid interest and turn it into your specialty

Got two sticks and some dirt? You can start yourself a fire. Have a skill set? You can be an expert. Expertise doesn't emerge overnight, naturally, but your path toward being the go-to guy can begin right now. Just look for ways to hone and improve skills you already have, turning something you've been doing as a matter of course into an elevated area of expertise.

The easiest way to stand out as a specialist is to look for a task or responsibility that has a clear practical value that others avoid and make it yours. Then get some advanced training or take a course that deepens your knowledge base and skills in your area. Say you're a sales rep with a basic proficiency in French. Take over the Canadian accounts, where your language skills can be a great asset. A young indoor street furniture ad sales agent I know who loved to shop took over the mall accounts no one else wanted and doubled sales for her firm.

Volunteer for as many assignments in your area of interest as you can to develop and market your expertise. It's not hard to become known as the go-to guy for a particular task if your colleagues know that you're always prepared to take it on and to do it better than anyone else would.

Stay ahead of any advancements in your area by continuing to experiment and refine your skills. If there's new technology associated with what you do, adopt and master it first. When you're the one who has the most advanced and expert knowledge in any critical area, when you have the elite skills the average Joe doesn't; when you're the sharpshooter—you're bulletproof.

▶ ▶ ▶ *Be a sharpshooter.*
▶ ▶ ▶ *Market your expert skills to your boss and coworkers.*

32. SHARE YOUR WORK

ShareNet, Google Docs, intranets, wikis. Oh, the power and majesty of technology-driven work sharing. Too bad all these fancy techno tools haven't actually taught us to be better sharers. Oh, sure, you'll post your presentations or files to share with your boss and your coworkers because you have to. But do you really have an open-source heart? Probably not. You're paranoid, and with good reason.

Work is a competition, and you are competing against your coworkers to keep your job. So while you must never give a colleague a good idea that might advance him in his job or cost you yours, if your company requires it, you have to be prepared to share your work.

Sharing your work is in the same scary category as sharing credit. You have to be willing to give up what you know to get something back. But you can't help wondering: Is it really safe to share? What if someone takes my ideas? What if they ridicule or

TRUE STORY

John worked for an interactive advertising agency whose CEO was addicted to in-house wiki-style document sharing. Every time a new project was launched, employees were expected to share feedback on working documents, adding insights, references, or resources regularly as the project evolved. John found the constant "sharing" to be a time-consuming pain in the ass that got in the way of his "real" work, so he just didn't bother. Imagine his surprise when he was cuffed at his job review for being "uncooperative" and "insubordinate" for being absent from his office's digital conversation. Now his name is at the top of every thread.

PAID TO SHARE

Some companies are so desperate to see knowledge exchanged that they're willing to give you a weekend in Vegas to prove it. A few years ago, Siemens, the multinational electronics and engineering conglomerate, challenged its workers to quit hoarding their information and expertise. It set up a knowledge-sharing network via ShareNet and invited employees to share their work with the entire global operation, making it available via chat, database, and search engine. The reward for successful sharing included cash bonuses for information that led to increased sales and perk-filled trips (viva Las Vegas!) for knowledge that proved valuable to someone else. You, of course, should be doing it to bulletproof your job.

tamper with my work? What if . . . oh, get over yourself! Just because you share your work doesn't mean people will actually use it or even look at it. Being willing to make it available is the meaningful gesture here. Call it the openly networked transfer of knowledge or call it pinning your shiny-gold-starred homework up on the bulletproof bulletin board, I don't care which.

Sharing information is both a social and a practical endeavor. It creates and sustains valuable connections between you and the people you work with and makes intellectual assets available that can help you all succeed. Plus, by the way, much of the work you do has a direct effect on other people's work, so if you don't share, you're not letting them do what they need to. The fact is that is more dangerous to hoard information than it is to share it freely.

Share your research, share your results, share your reports, share your insights. Share anything that will be of value to your colleagues—without giving away the store, of course. Think of it as an advertisement for the smoking hot work you're capable of doing. Understand that the threat to you as a result of sharing *what your company is paying you to create* is minimal. And the benefits include your looking not just smart but generous and confident *and* smart.

▶▶▶ *Don't hoard information.*

33. TAKE RESPONSIBILITY

Someone who doesn't take responsibility for his work or his actions or his relationships is a dodger. He has no concept of the word "accountability" and when the shit hits the fan, he is usually nowhere to be found. Dodging responsibility is an *extremely* unattractive behavior, one that no one will cut you slack on or forgive you for or volunteer to help you change.

The dodger is the weasel who says, "Who, me?" when the boss is looking for someone to own up to a missed deadline, a disappointed client, or lagging sales, and the good guy is the one who raises his hand and says, "Me, that's mine, my bad." In this case, you definitely want to be the good guy.

Now, I'm not telling you to run around taking the blame for a bunch of random mistakes because that's not a very clever way to bulletproof your job, is it? I'm just telling you to take full responsibility for your work in the first place, from top to bottom, start to finish. Because when you truly own your work—the successes *and* the mistakes—the mistakes tend to happen rarely and the successes become the norm. Why is that?

When you take responsibility for your work, you learn to treat your job as if it's your own little business, for which you're

BEFORE YOU BLAME ME, TAKE A LOOK AT YOURSELF

For most people, avoiding responsibility starts with a voice in their heads that points out the faults of others so that they don't have to face their own. Over time, blaming other people or dismissing all circumstances as "factors beyond my control" becomes the default, and before you know it, you've lived a whole life determined—in your mind—by the vagaries of fate and the cruel or mistaken actions of others. Pitiful! The first step toward taking responsibility of the outcomes of your own life is to stop blaming everyone else. Here's how to quit playing the blame game.

▶ Listen to yourself. Keep a record for a day of all the times you fault someone or something else. You're late for work because of that jackass in front of you at the light. You missed your conference call because the receptionist didn't come and find you in the coffee room. That damn printer was acting up, and now there's a page missing from your report. Note the excuses you give to others, as well as the thoughts you keep to yourself.

If you're a chronic blamer and you're honest with yourself and observant when you do this exercise, you'll no doubt end up with an appallingly long list of complaints against others. Hmmm. I don't know about you, but I wouldn't leave my job security in the hands of a bunch of jackasses and receptionists and printers. When you choose to own your outcomes instead of blaming them on others, you begin to see all the ways you can control those outcomes and make them turn out better.

on the hook for every outcome. When you take responsibility for your choices, your actions, the direction of your work, and the quality of your work relationships, you can finally under-

▶ Look in the mirror. Every time you catch yourself blaming someone—whether silently to yourself or, worse, out loud—stop and identify your own role in the outcome. Then identify an alternative behavior that would have changed the result. You left the house late and the jackass at the light only made you later. Leave five minutes earlier every day, and the lights won't matter. The receptionist forgot her crystal ball and didn't know you were in the coffee room when your call came in because you didn't tell her. If you're important enough to be on a conference call, be responsible enough to be at your phone at the assigned time. And you can't change the @#%##$# printer, can you? So give yourself time to proofread your print job, so when you discover that a page is missing, you have a chance to fix it. 99.9 percent of the time you'll discover that an infinitely better outcome is in *your* control.

▶ Ask someone for feedback. Nothing is a louder wake-up call than when a trusted friend or family member confirms that yes, you do have a blame problem. Of course, your reaction when they tell you this might be to blame them! Get past that, though, and know that everything you do to eliminate this behavior and replace it with taking responsibility for your own actions will make you stronger, better, more bulletproof.

stand what that plaque on President Truman's desk meant: "The buck stops here." No passing blame, no pawning off excuses. When you succeed, it's your success. When you don't, well, that's yours, too.

You learn to take responsibility because you don't want to be a dodger. Even though a dodger can be resourceful in a sneaky sort of way, cleverly sticking blame on others' backs like a "Kick

JUST SO YOU KNOW

"I'm just the messenger" is shorthand for not taking responsibility for your part in a difficult conversation you find yourself having. And though it seems like an effective way to insulate yourself from a negative reaction, you're actually calling yourself out as being unable or unwilling to be responsible for the information you're sharing. People hate "the messenger" when he's bearing bad news, so why would you ever refer to yourself as one? It's not always easy, but it's much safer in the long run to take responsibility for what you're saying every time.

me" sign, smart bosses can smell a dodger a mile away and will open the nearest trapdoor and give him a shove. Even dumb bosses eventually catch on to a dodger's shirking ways.

Dodgers are a terrible burden on morale and productivity in the workplace. So taking responsibility is a bulletproof tactic you can begin to benefit from right now.

▶▶▶ *Own the outcome of all your actions and decisions.*
▶▶▶ *Don't blame others and don't make excuses.*

34. TAKE INITIATIVE

Initiative is the glue that holds together everything else you're doing to bulletproof your job. It asks you to call on your flexibility, your utility, and your specialties, to name a few. The ability to take initiative is one of the greatest qualities a person can possess, yet it is rare in the best of times and almost nonexistent when things get tough. Why? Because taking initiative is scary. It requires the motivation, courage, and confidence to make the first move and to do something without being asked. It necessitates being flexible, taking responsibility, being creative and skilled.

Because we know that everything that happens at Homer Simpson's job is absurdly true to life, it's easy to see why a person would seek invisibility over prominence, subsistence over success. Because taking initiative always means taking on more and lots of us spend our work lives looking for less, not more. And because *not* raising your hand and saying "I'll do it!" is so much easier than raising your hand and risking failure.

In spite of all the perceived risk, taking initiative is probably the best, most worthwhile thing you can do to prove your worth at work—*especially* during a rough spell. Even the highest-level managers are afraid to make a wrong move, and behaviors across the organization can become cautious to the point of being paralyzed. That's why such times are a golden opportunity to add value when it's needed most by taking initiative.

TRUE STORY

Michelle was a low-level supervisor in the corporate office of a large retail chain. Business was dramatically down, and she knew many jobs in her department weren't safe, including her own. So she quickly put together a series of projects for her department to improve its bottom line (see number 38, "Add dollar value"), which everyone eagerly signed up for, hoping to protect their own jobs. No one asked her to do this, and she didn't know for sure her scheme would work. But she showed a fearless initiative— nothing to lose, right?—and rallied the troops. In the end, four jobs were eliminated in her department, but not Michelle's. And when the economy recovered and the business improved along with it, she got a fat promotion.

Yes, when you raise your hand, you might be wrong. Sure, when you take a first step, you might make a mistake. But initiative gives the atmosphere a shot of movement and motion and progress and promise that creates a positive momentum that always trumps short-term errors. You will be remembered for going above and beyond to solve a problem or to chase a prospect. And, more important, for inspiring everyone around you to get moving, too. The example of taking initiative is hard to ignore.

So how can you cultivate the desire to take a chance, ask for more, and push yourself and others beyond your comfort zone?

▶ Answer a ringing phone. Make a point of doing things that need to be done, even if it's "not your job." Anticipate a need and meet it, even if that's just picking up a Starbucks for your boss without being asked. Pitching in without being asked is a contagious behavior.

▶ Raise your hand. Volunteer for challenging projects—especially the ones everyone else wants to avoid. Offer to take on unpopular tasks or to try to solve a tricky problem. Every situation your deadbeat coworkers say "No, thank you" to is an opportunity for you to show initiative.

▶ Move swiftly. Don't delay making decisions, taking action, moving forward, or even stepping back when necessary. The enemy of initiative is procrastination.

▶ Play small ball. Taking initiative doesn't always require throwing yourself on a live grenade or performing other heroic acts. Every exchange or task is an opportunity to take initiative in a multitude of small ways.

▶ Own the outcome. Taking initiative requires being brave and committed enough to take the first step, but then also following up with lots of other steps that can be hard and risky and are not guaranteed to work every time. Take every step prepared to succeed but strong enough to fail and to take responsibility for the outcome no matter which way it goes. Then move quickly to the next outcome. And the next.

▶ Bring others along. Invite coworkers to make the first move with you. Do it by example, do it by request. Build a team of initiative takers who will solve problems, create opportunities, and add value when your company needs it most. Your collective success will make your team members of your sleeper cell of supporters.

▶▶▶ *Make taking initative second nature.*
▶▶▶ *Learn to roll with the risk required when you take initiative.*

35. SUPPORT YOUR BOSS

This is one of the tactics for bulletproofing your job that I like the best. It's incredibly effective, and you can do it in an infinite number of ways. In polite circles, it's called "supporting" your boss, but really it's just sucking up.

Obsequious, sure, But it's also nuts-and-bolts practical. It boils down to understanding that having good chemistry with your boss is the most important thing you can do to bulletproof your job. Good chemistry starts with paying attention to what your boss needs, how she operates, what she likes and doesn't like—and then shaping your attitude and approach to your work to reflect that. Hear me now: Your boss *is* your job. So get this right, will you?

First, you have to get to know your boss *personally*. This re-

ASK YOURSELF:

▶ Do I know what my boss needs?

▶ Do I reflect his style?

▶ Do I represent his goals in my work?

▶ Does he know he can count on me to get the job done the way he would want it?

▶ Does my boss even *like* me?

quires that you quietly ignore the invisible barriers to "getting personal" that are suggested by HR and company handbooks and general personnel policy and go right ahead and be conscious of taking in personal details about your boss such as information about her family, kids, hobbies, education, previous jobs, and so on as these things come up in conversation. What subjects is she enthusiastic about? And what is she sensitive about? Note her habits, such as when she comes in the morning (or afternoon) and when she leaves in the afternoon (or morning!). Observe her style, such as whether she's hands-on or hands-off, warm and engaging or cool and distant, detail-oriented or a macro manager. Is she in the thick of office politics or a process wonk? All of this information will help *you* make *her* look good. I mean support her, of course.

To be clear, cultivating good chemistry is *your* job, not your boss's. *You* make all the observations and adjustments and efforts so that the relationship is successful. But even though you're doing all the heavy lifting in the relationship, at the same time, you can control your own agenda and get what you need to pave a path toward success and security. Keep your boss's agenda ahead of your own—and work like the devil to help him achieve it.

Here are the rules:

▶ Adapt to your boss's style. This is what I have referred to previously as being a Mini Me. However she likes to communicate—how often, in what format, to what level of detail—that's what you like too. Whatever her pace throughout the day, that's yours, too. You should even be faintly mimicking her personal style; if she has an Ivy League flair, you should lose the chunky platforms and leather jacket. Don't worry, you won't end up as the Smithers to your boss's Mr. Burns. You're just positioning

JUST SO YOU KNOW

While being a Mini Me has its obvious advantages, there's nothing wrong with exploiting the differences you have with your boss. In fact, smart bosses sometimes hire you because of your differences, not in spite of them. Opposites do attract, and if you happen to deduce that you are, in fact, your boss's antithesis, it's probably not that you deceived him in the interview, but rather that he has shortcomings in areas where he suspected you were particularly strong.

Example: I am disorganized, inappropriate, street smart more than book smart, and I bring my personal life to the office all the time. (Good thing I'm the boss, eh?) I hired Sean because he's smart, he has impeccable skills, he's discreet, and he's quiet. I barely know a thing about his personal life—and not, I might add, for lack of trying! But unlike me, he's careful to create boundaries, is polite and perfectly appropriate, and makes me look good. He's the Ugly Betty to my Daniel Meade—we couldn't be more different on the outside, but we're pursuing my goals in tandem.

JUST SO YOU KNOW

You should be the first to know what's up with your boss, whether he tells you about it or not. That's why you need to set up Google and Yahoo! alerts for your boss's name and your company's name to be delivered to your private e-mail address at home.

Don't you want to know if he's been picked up for DUI while visiting his mother in Florida? Or whether there are rumors of your company being sold? Of course you do. And while you're at it, use Technorati to monitor what's being said about your company in the blogosphere.

yourself to give her exactly what she needs and tucking into her tailwind so you can get what you need, too. (That's job security, of course, but also the opportunity to grow.)

▶ Manage expectations. Do not promise your boss anything you can't provide, such as delivering a report on a subject you know nothing about or a client you can't get. Just because he's yelling and demanding something doesn't mean it's possible for you to deliver it. While it's tempting to just say "Yes, of course, right away, sir!," in the end, you're setting yourself up to disappoint and displease. Instead, tell him exactly what you *can* do and then get to work on a strategy to get him the rest.

▶ Be a stickler for clarification. Lots of bosses know what they want but aren't very good at expressing it. If you're not 100 percent crystal clear on what she's expecting, ask questions. She may be annoyed that you're badgering her for details, but she'll be a lot more annoyed if you walk in with a red prototype when she wanted blue.

▶ Be a master of the logistics of your relationship. As noted earlier, you're in charge of this working relationship. In a way, you become your boss's secret boss—you become the wife or mother of your relationship. (I know, I shock myself sometimes.) So *you* manage the details. If you don't, no one else will.

▶ Underpromise and overdeliver. Every single time. I cannot emphasize enough how important this is. This is how you control your boss's perception of you as a can-do winner rather than the unfortunate opposite of that. Seize every opportunity to surprise him with an extra dash of excellence. This is where you make him look so good, it becomes a habit he can't shake. That's right, he's jonesing for it. And he's sure not going to fire it.

▶ Cultivate a good impression among people your boss respects. Obviously, start with *his* boss. Then move on to that marketing director with whom your boss has a great rapport and whose opinions are golden in his eyes. If they like you or think you do good work, it will elevate you in your boss's eyes.

▶▶▶ **Be your boss's Mini Me.**
▶▶▶ **Cultivate excellent chemistry between you and your boss.**
▶▶▶ **Take control of the success of your relationship with your boss.**

36. LEND A HAND

When times are tough, there's nothing more welcome than someone asking, "How can I help?" It leaves a nice, long-lasting impression on the folks who make the who-stays/who-goes decisions, too.

Think of this as extra credit at work. It shouldn't take away from the responsibilities that are already on your plate, but when

JUST SO YOU KNOW

To be perfectly clear, you should lend a hand when there's a bulletproof benefit; either you'll get valuable brownie points with your boss, or you know that the person you help will join your sleeper cell of supporters and return the favor someday. Work isn't a charity, and if you spend your time helping every schlub who needs it, you boss is going to think you have too much time on your hands. Dole out assistance in your company or within your industry only for future return; spending your precious "help" chits on your oafish roommate from college doesn't fall within that definition.

you have a free hand and someone else needs it, reach out. It's worth it.

First, make sure you're helping someone who deserves it, not one of those slackers who never gets his work done on time or who handicaps himself by never becoming competent with his systems or computer programs. In this case, Darwin was right. It's survival of the fittest, and these dopes need a little taste of extinction to set them straight, not a bailout from you.

Help a guy who never asks for help. Help a guy who has helped you before. Help a newbie who's in over his head. You may just be doing ditch digging to help them plow through. Copying, collating, word processing a chimp could do. Regardless, make no judgment about the kind of work, just make yourself available to do what needs doing. Unlike a shirker, who, besides abject laziness and ineptitude suffers from chronic amnesia, these *deserving* folks will never forget your assistance and will turn up more than once to return the favor.

The bulletproof question, of course, is what's the benefit to you, other than the warm, self-satisfied, superhero feeling you get when you've convinced yourself you saved the day? Well, none, unless you make your efforts known to someone who matters. Like your boss and the other bosslike people in your work life, who will appreciate seeing how useful you are. Here are some subtle ways to share the good news:

- ▶ If you're already in the habit of submitting reports and summaries of your work to your supervisor, slip a mention of your extra credit in there.
- ▶ Give the person you helped public credit for getting a tough job done. This graciously, subtly implies your involvement and shared credit for the accomplishment (see number 26, "Share credit"). Send a little "Atta boy"/"Good for us" e-mail around or say something nice to your boss/his boss about what a good job he did.
- ▶ As with all of the project work you do, inside and outside your scope of responsibility, document your efforts in your own records (see number 40, "Keep your resume current"). You never know when the details might come in handy.

▶▶▶ *Have a reputation for being willing and able to help.*
▶▶▶ *Offer help freely but choose whom you help wisely.*

37. WORK HARD

You want to say, "Well, duh!" to this one, but I won't let you. That's because you'd be shocked to know how many people don't realize they need to ramp it up and pump it out when the going gets tough. Some people get paralyzed with anxiety about

THE DIFFERENCE BETWEEN WORK AND HARD WORK

▶ There's more of it. Hard work is the result of pushing for that extra 20 percent output.

▶ It requires your full focus. A quick ramp-up and then sustained attention until you're done, with no distractions.

▶ Doing it now versus doing it later. Regular work often features dawdling and procrastination. Hard work has a pressing urgency built into it. Every. Single. Time.

▶ Doing it right versus getting it done. You don't rush to get something done; rather, you pace yourself to do it properly. Hard work has a higher standard.

the unknown and, instead of pitching in to save the burning barn, they stand there gaping at it with an empty bucket in their hands.

Let's be honest with ourselves. Most of us don't know the meaning of hard work. That's what our grandfathers did, building stone walls by hand or pulling double shifts at the factory. We think a few late nights or the occasional Saturday at the office makes us workaholics. Hardly.

I'm not suggesting that it's the amount of time you spend at work that counts. It's the combination of quantity and quality of work you produce—especially compared to the people you work with—that reflects your value as an employee. Your hard work isn't so easy to appreciate when times are flush and HR can't hire worker bees fast enough to spread the tasks around. But when belts are being tightened, your work ethic and productivity are on full display, so take advantage of the opportunity.

Today, employees come in five varieties.

1. Those who work hard, go the extra mile, and don't complain.

2. Those who work hard and complain.

3. Those who coast and shirk.

4. Those whose boss is their mommy or daddy.

5. Those who are sleeping with the boss.

Types 2 and 3 will be fired. Types 4 and 5 will not. And Type 1, well, that has to be you.

What does hard work look like? Deadlines that are met no matter what, expectations that are exceeded at all times, a pronounced absence of procrastination, an obvious purpose and momentum to your efforts, and asking yourself at least once a day, "What else can I do?" No one should ever see you checking an auction on eBay because you had a few "free minutes." There's no such thing as free time at work.

Even if you are working hard, you need to be doing a whole lot more than that to bulletproof your job (see numbers 1 to 36 and 38 to 50). So let's just say it's the *least* you should be doing.

▶▶▶ *Be known as the one who works harder than anyone else.*
▶▶▶ *Show vigor and doggedness to get the job done.*

38. ADD DOLLAR VALUE

This is the one bulletproof tactic that is likely to save you even when you're doing everything else wrong. And don't be so quick to say this is easier said than done. *Anyone* can find a way to help cut costs or increase revenue at work. It's like finding money and handing it over to your boss. I know *I'd* hesitate to fire even a complete idiot if he was putting cash in my pocket. Results are results.

I'm not talking about discovering gold or inventing the next Post-it. You don't have the time or the resources for that, and neither does anyone else when they're fighting to stay afloat. It really is as basic as finding a way to pinch some pennies or identify or improve a source of revenue that doesn't require a capital investment. When money's tight at home, what do you do? You clip coupons, you quit going out to dinner, you have yard sales, you get rid of your expensive toys, you carpool to work. On the

TRUE STORY

Every year, Sarah, an HR executive, got her boss to sign off on a conference she liked to attend to learn "leadership skills." This outing usually cost a couple thousand dollars, but because the expense was mostly underwritten by an outside sponsor, Sarah always put in her request and always got to go. One year, though, her company was slogging through a long, slow stretch in a sagging economy, and budget cuts were rampant. Her boss turned her down and eventually turned her out. Money wasn't the issue; it was the fact that Sarah didn't understand how bad it looked to be asking to go on a three-day leadership training cruise (!) when budgets were being cut across the company.

job, you can find all kinds of ways to make similar adjustments that will benefit the bottom line. That's that magic number your boss is responsible for, and any way you can help him improve it makes him look good. Reminder: that's your most important job in good times or bad, to make the boss look good.

So it's up to you to ferret out the creative ways to skinflint and scrimp on costs and scavenge and forage for revenue. And then present them to your boss with a flourish and take a bow. Below are some ideas that are by no means exhaustive, but they'll help you see that there are all kinds of trails to scout.

First of all, the best way add value to the bottom line is to protect it. Essentially, that means doing everything you can to keep your current clients or customers supersatisfied so they don't go away. And while you can't take as much credit for that as for finding new sources of dough, it behooves you to do whatever you can to help your company keep its current customers happy. In bumpy times, they're what keeps your company afloat.

In the coupon-clipping category, look for material costs and expenses that can be cut. Start with any expenses for which you're personally accountable, such as charges to an expense account or work you'd normally send out that you might be able to handle in-house. If you're familiar enough with your department's budget, have a good look at it and brainstorm some possibilities. If not, look around you. Your company doesn't really need to provide that expensive Costa Rican coffee for free right now, does it? Think like your mother—I guarantee you'll find some quarters under the couch cushions.

Look for ways to share expenses with synergistic, noncompetitive companies: advertising, office space, even employees you don't want to let go. If you uncover opportunities like these that pan out, your boss will love your ass.

Think of a new way to sell your company's stuff. Can you reposition your products or services or bundle them differently to appeal to a different kind of customer, perhaps one with a smaller budget? For example, if you usually market your services developing customer surveys for your clients for a flat fee, think about offering them on an hourly basis to attract new interest.

Participate in brainstorming a new marketing plan. When business is slow, you have the time to focus on marketing that you (mistakenly) weren't spending when business was busy. Even if you're not a marketing type, it's a good time to think like one. All fresh ideas will be welcomed.

Revisit old opportunities. As I've said before, good times are bad for you at work. You forget how to jump on every lead and extract every ounce of value out of it. Lean times should make you rethink your business model. Go back to opportunities you didn't pursue (perhaps they seemed too small in the old, robust economy) and see if you can get any of them going again.

Get your existing clients to help you discover new opportunities. Your satisfied current customers can be your best source of new leads. Identify the best possibilities, and court their influence. And treat them extra nice (see above re taking care of the customers you already have).

▶▶▶ *Help your company save money or find new ways to make money.*
▶▶▶ *Be noticeably frugal.*

BULLETPROOF TAKEAWAY

Being useful takes a commitment that bumps you out of your cozy (lazy?) comfort zone and into a kind of do-do-do mode that's a lot like your mother bustling around the house cooking and cleaning and making those little pilgrim hat place cards the day before Thanksgiving. It's not busy work, but it sure keeps her busy. It's the same kind of admirable, energetic industry that your boss should think of every time he looks at you.

I've pointed you to a bunch of ways to step up and be the poster child for hard work and diligence:

▶ Volunteer to mentor or train coworkers. Don't be stingy about sharing your work or lending a hand.

▶ Offer unique skills as well as a broadly useful skill set. Take initiative and be responsible for your work.

▶ Make your boss look good, add dollar value, and work your ass off.

All you have to do is look around your workplace to see that there's a lot to be done. Bulletproof your job by being the one your boss sees doing it.

4

BE READY

If you think of bulletproofing your job in terms of increased visibility, greater accessibility, and utility as the flashy-dashy cosmetic stuff, being ready is more like flossing your teeth. Not flashy. Not even very noticeable, unless, of course, you're *not* doing it. But absolutely critical to having a day-to-day mind-set that keeps you prepared for any eventuality. When you're ready for anything, you behave with a certainty that you'll succeed when all is well and land on your feet if you hit a bump in the road.

While being visible, easy, and useful relates to specific tactics and behaviors you should adopt in the context of your *job*, being ready encompasses tactics focused on the long-term maintenance of your *career*. And though I have always maintained that your career *is* your job and vice versa, from a bulletproof perspective, it's the point at which your short-term goal (keeping the job you have) and your long-term objectives (making a steady living and a steady progression upward in responsibility, position, and income no matter what the job climate) intersect. Pursuing the short-term goal without keeping the long-term one also in mind may not build job security that will carry you into the future. In other words, sure, you're dodging a bullet now, but you'll probably keel over from heart disease tomorrow.

Being ready gives you confidence, and confidence gives you presence, which is attractive to everyone. Colleagues will gravitate toward you as if in a trance, and even your boss will be swayed by your influence. **Confidence creates a powerful force field around you that protects you from immediate as well as future threats and challenges.**

39. HAVE MONEY IN THE BANK

One of the single most important things you can do to bulletproof your job is to have money in the bank—a bare minimum of six months' worth of living expenses, readily available in a CD or other liquid savings vehicle, not to be touched for vacations or handbags or cosmetic procedures or anything. If you're over 40, make that a year's worth of expenses socked away, and if you're over 50, you're looking at more like two years. (Sorry, but ageism exists and the older you are, the longer it will take you to land a job.) These are the amounts advised by financial experts that should be reserved to tide you over in case you lose your job. So how will this bulletproof the job you have?

Money equals confidence. Knowing your rent or mortgage is covered in any event will allow you to behave with a strategic long-term interest in keeping your job, taking care of your boss, and serving your company, not out of desperation to get the next paycheck. When money is taken out of the immediate equation,

STASHING THE CASH

Setting aside six months' worth of expenses may seem like a bear of a challenge at first, and no one likes to cinch the belt in ways that make one feel, well, poor. But it's better to feel a little poor while you're building your bank account than to feel a lot poor if you get the heave-ho and have nothing to fall back on. I'm not going to tell you how to pinch your pennies; you know how much you spend on music or cabs or top-shelf cocktails or expensive gadgets. Do what dieters do: keep a log of everything you're "consuming" and start cutting things out. So forgive me for sounding like your mother—again—but if you eliminate just a few expenses each month, your savings will add up swiftly.

you won't avoid doing all the other things you need to do to bulletproof your job that might otherwise have seemed too risky—such as speaking up or taking initiative or sharing credit. You'll be less likely to hold back in doing what's necessary to *keep* your job when you aren't financially afraid of *losing* your job.

Having money in the bank also gives you options. Even though your number-one goal is to protect the job you have, knowing you could walk out the door if you had to and still pay your bills should give you a secret sense of security and an open air of self-sufficiency and pride that suggests you are sure of your abilities and locked in for the long haul. A girl who knows she's got a black book full of guys who want to go out with her exudes a self-assuredness that's like catnip to every other guy. Use your financial security to make you feel like a million bucks' worth of confidence every time you sit down at your desk at work.

Having money socked away also allows you to explore other career options at the appropriate time, whether that means tak-

ASK YOURSELF:

As you update your resume, take a step back and evaluate it from the reader's perspective. Make sure you're putting your best foot forward. Ask yourself:

- ▶ Is it easy to identify each past employer, the dates of employment, and my job responsibilities?

- ▶ Is it clear what kind of job I'd like next?

- ▶ Do the job responsibilities I've listed demonstrate my qualifications for the job I want next?

- ▶ Do I use action verbs?

- ▶ Have I highlighted key accomplishments?

ing another job, changing careers, going back to school, or starting your own business. In the long term, your career may benefit more from a new experience than from staying right where you are. Having money in the bank will set you up to make the leap to where you want to be when you're ready to make it.

A final word. Every time the economy starts to frown, I tell everyone to put away their credit cards. Even if you're not in debt, now's not the time to get that way. It's the time to shore up and be as financially secure as you can be for any eventuality. And if you are in debt, get serious about getting out of it. Forget your usual extravagant Christmas gifts or anything else that gets you in deeper. And take advantage of the economic downturn to refinance your debt at more favorable terms.

▶▶▶ **Be financially prepared to weather the unexpected storm.**

▶▶▶ **Eliminate personal debt when the economy gets iffy.**

40. KEEP YOUR RESUME CURRENT

The best time to update your resume is when you're not actively looking for a new position. Polishing it up regularly will ensure that you always have a sharp resume at the ready and will put you in a better position to pursue new opportunities that come up quickly, without necessitating that you do a major overhaul to reflect the past few years of your career.

Every sixty days or so, pull out your resume and check to see that your current position is accurately described. Have you added any new responsibilities that should be included? Acquired any new skills or certifications? Met any notable goals or received kudos for particular achievements? Although they may

YOUR DOSSIER

Your HR department has a personnel file on you that contains your resume, performance reviews, and other kudos and warnings, but what do you have in the dossier you keep for yourself? Set up a career file that contains your resume, copies of certificates and awards, letters of congratulation and thanks, and anything else that remotely resembles a pat on the back, also known as "success documents." Save your "fan letters" and go back to the writers later to ask them to be a reference. Having notes to remind you and them of what makes you so stupendous can be a helpful starting point.

be clear in your mind today, if you put off updating your resume too long, you may have trouble quantifying your achievements or remembering *exactly* when you were promoted.

And don't forget to take a step back and consider that, over time, your career goals may have changed, too. Your resume should reflect that. If you started out in marketing but have since discovered that sales is your passion, for example, make sure your resume points up your sales successes, even the small ones. If you aspire to be a senior executive, revise your resume to show-case your leadership and management triumphs, not necessarily your hands-on skills. What you include—and don't include—on your resume should lead readers to see a fit between the job you want and the background you're describing.

As you add new skills and experiences, make sure you also de-lete older or irrelevant jobs. In general, anything over fifteen years old should be removed or downplayed, unless there is a particular experience that is helpful to highlight. That might in-clude a leadership role, experience directly relevant to the type of job you'd like to have next, or an award that makes you uniquely qualified for a position. You can go ahead and take out facts like the high school you attended and your college GPA, especially if you're over age 25. Being chairman of the social committee of your fraternity was probably a blast, but your future boss doesn't need to know about it.

In that vein, if you possess garden-variety computer skills—say a basic proficiency with Microsoft Office applications, don't bother to mention them if you're out of the entry-level sphere. If you have distinguished skills in this area—say, using a sophisti-cated accounting program—go right ahead and brag about it. If you're junior level, note it on your resume. If you're senior level, mention it at the appropriate moment should you interview for a new position. And if you're junior level aspiring to senior level, find a way to brag about it without noting it on your resume. Otherwise you'll stay at the junior level thanks to the search-and-sort feature of automated resume review programs.

Finally, be sure to bring your up-to-date resume to every job review. Explain to your supervisor that you think it's helpful to the review process to refresh memories about your job history. You'd be surprised how surprised *he* might be to see the ways you're building up your skills and experience as reflected in your resume. It's always helpful for your boss to see how far you've come and how valuable you are—right there in black and white. As an aside, knowing you have a sharp, current resume may make your boss a little nervous—the good kind of nervous, the kind that makes him want to protect his investment in his valuable employee.

You should also share your up-to-date resume with a new boss or a supervisor who is new to your department. It's an effective way of introducing yourself and giving her a clear picture of your professional background and a good idea what you're capable of. Make it clear that you're sharing as a courtesy, the CliffsNotes on you that will save the new boss the trouble of figuring out who and what you are.

▶▶▶ *Be ready with an excellent, up-to-the-minute resume at all times.*

▶▶▶ *Keep a thorough file of success documents to support your resume.*

41. ESTABLISH A RELATIONSHIP WITH A RECRUITER

As with keeping up your resume, initiating a relationship with a recruiter is best done when you're *not* looking for a job. That's because when you really need his or her professional assistance, you don't want to start cold. Having a good rapport with a headhunter long before you may need to call on him or her for their active services is your best bulletproof defense and your best offense for the future.

First, let's be clear about the dynamic about here. A recruiter works for client companies that are looking to fill positions. That's right, he works for *them,* not for *you.* In that way, a recruiter is like a real estate agent; you're the buyer, and he represents the seller. When a real estate agent sells you a house, he is paid by the seller. Likewise, a headhunter is paid by the hiring company to fill a position, *not* to find you a job. This doesn't mean a recruiter won't be a useful contact in the short and long terms or that he won't pull out the stops on your behalf if you're a great candidate for a job he's trying to fill. It just means he has his clients at the top of his agenda, not you.

That said, if you get a relationship going with a savvy recruiter who specializes in your field, someone with whom you really click, it can be a supremely beneficial connection. Specifically, when he becomes aware of a great job that would suit you perfectly, he'll think of you first. Good for you, good for him, everybody wins.

The best recruiter for you will know your field well, know his client companies well, and be well acquainted with the details of the jobs he's charged with filling. He won't be tempted to make a less-than-perfect match because he benefits only when

JUST SO YOU KNOW

As an executive recruiter, I have a world of respect for all kinds of professionals in the career field, from HR representatives to employment counselors to resume consultants and more. It's the idea of a "career coach" that I don't get. Coaches are for Little League. Why not just find a decent shrink or a good bartender? Hiring someone to coach you about your career is like paying a friend to give you advice. It's silly to think of a grown adult needing to be coached through anything. It suggests a kind of immaturity and insecurity that I find offputting. I mean, what would you do if your 45-year-old heart surgeon told you he was working with a "cardiac coach" to give him advice about your surgery? Scary. It's time to grow up, figure out what you're good at, and do it.

his matches are successful for both the employer and the employee. He must also be someone you trust, with whom you have a good personal chemistry, and whose intelligence and instincts you admire. So how can you find this dream date?

There are contingency headhunters, who are paid a fee only after filling a position for a client. Retainer-based recruiters are paid incrementally to screen and present well-qualified candidates for a position or a variety of positions on behalf of client companies. Both types specialize in particular industries, so start by finding the right ones for your line of work. Note that retainer-based recruiters will rarely interview you if they don't have a particular assignment to which you would be well suited, so don't be insulted if they refuse.

Recruiting is an industry fueled by information—gossip, to be precise. Inside scoop about people leaving jobs or being fired, new positions being created, reorganizations. So once you've met a recruiter you like, the best way to stay on her radar is to be a good source of news, candidates for jobs she's trying to fill, and potential clients for her. That way, when you're in the market for a job or she has something that's a good opportunity for you, you'll be at the top of the list of people to call.

▶▶▶ *Make friends with a headhunter in your field.*

42. IMPROVE YOUR NETWORKING SKILLS

Just a few decades ago, a network was one of the three channels you watched on television. Now it's a verb and an immeasurably vital part of bulletproofing your job in the short and long terms. At its most basic level, networking is about proactively putting yourself in a position to meet (and get to know!) people who may ultimately be able to impact your career. Simply put, job survival and advancement are about always having a substantial list of professional acquaintances. Networking is also a state of mind—a kind of ongoing openness to the possibility that the person you've just met on the elevator or in line at a restaurant could be your next client or even your new boss. And being in that state of mind—at all times—is the part of networking that's crucial to getting and keeping a job.

So you avoid networking because you're a little uncomfortable with mixing and mingling with people you've never met before? Good. It's supposed to push you out of your comfort zone and make you reach and be creative in the way you interact with people. Be the one who offers a Viagra handshake first in an introduction (see number 12). Be the one who engages in conversation that goes beyond "Hi, how are you doing?" Be the one who sets goals to meet new people wherever you go. Networking is, at heart, about making connections that will have a long-term, often unexpected, value as you move through your career.

What exactly is this network you're building? A wide variety of people, including those who are in your field and industry, as well as others in a related fields, unrelated fields, perhaps people who share your interests outside the workplace, even people you randomly meet in the course of your day-to-day life. The most influential and useful are usually those who work in and around your field, but it's not at all unusual for an outsider to be the most effective person in your network. That's because network-ing is only partly about what someone does for a living; the rest is what kind of person he is and how good he is at being a con-nector.

You probably think you're networking when you go to a con-ference and collect a handful of business cards. Those are just cards, not people. You have to dig deeper than that, get to know the person whose card you're holding, and determine if she is someone you could reach out to—and of course someone you might help as well. It's true that you can't know for sure if some-one will be a fruitful contact at first meeting, but you can gather plenty of clues from a first conversation and store them up for later. And when you follow up on that first meeting—which is a *must*—you can probe a little further and determine whether it's worth investing time and attention on this person.

Send a nice-to-meet-you e-mail and a reminder of what you discussed. If proximity allows, arrange a lunch or drinks to begin to deepen the connection if it continues to seem promising. And stay in touch, even with just a once-a-month "What's up?" or bits of news he might be interested in. Just don't waste a good

LINK UP

Facebook, LinkedIn, and other profession-specific social networking sites are an important way to share news, professional insights, and contact information with people in your field. Powerful, personal, and lasting connections can be made in these venues, where people often feel freer to share opinions and swap tales from the trenches. Mistakes can be made, too, when you feel too comfortable just being you among your professional peers. So set up a smart, slick page that puts your best "you" out there. Putting up inappropriate personal information about yourself almost always causes more harm than good, in innumerable ways, not the least of which being that if your employer gets a look at it, you could be sacked. In fact, employers are using these networking pages to check out what their employees are "up to," so leave off the beer pong pix from your trip to Cabo. Really.

connection by not taking care of it once it's established. If you do, when you try to reach out for help when you need it, the connection won't be there.

Be mindful that networking is a two-way street. For every person you collect into your network because she may be helpful to you, you should count on being called on to be a resource for her, too. So when you are considering the value of someone in your network, consider also whether you'd be inclined to give back. Don't be reluctant to let an acquaintance languish that lacks chemistry or value. There's such a thing as stretching your network too thin.

Networking *isn't* going out for cocktails with your colleagues after work and griping about your boss. You have to put yourself in new places where you have better-than-average odds of aug-

menting your list of most-favored persons. Professional association meetings, business conferences, college alumni gatherings,
and work-related events and dinners are no-brainers. So whereas
you might have turned down these kinds of opportunities in the
past in favor of that hot-rock spinning class you love, if you're serious about bulletproofing, you gotta go to these functions.
Showing up is the first step. The rest is what you make of it.

Networking is a huge part of what I do every day, and I have a
few "musts" I follow religiously. I always add new acquaintances
to my contacts immediately after I meet them. I make a point of
seeing them again in person for a drink or coffee within two
months of meeting them, if they're local. And if they're long distance, I e-mail to follow up. I press myself to meet at least six
new people at every event I attend. And I never drink alcohol at
events. Teetotaling for two hours is easy; making up for two hours
of networking opportunities you missed by not staying sharp is
hard.

Once at an event, don't be a stiff, standing off in a corner by
yourself or hanging out with your buddies all night. If you're not
reaching out to strangers, you're not networking. Instead, introduce yourself to people who are by themselves, perhaps not
knowing anyone in the room. Ask them their names, where they
work, what they do, where they live, who you might know in
common (see numbers 11 and 12, "Grow your circle" and "Introduce yourself"). Take responsibility for getting the conversation
going, and then try to expand your twosome to three or more, so
that everyone benefits from getting to know one another. Practice your personal pitch (see number 12, "Introduce yourself"),
and pay attention to their pitches, too. Having a good pitch is a
good clue that a person is an interesting prospect for your network.

MY OWN TRUE STORY

Sometimes all of your worlds happily collide when you're a networking monster like me. The book you hold in your hands is an example of that. I first met the senior executive at HarperCollins who acquired this book years ago, when she was a producer for a major morning television show where I worked as a career expert. When the proposal for this book was being circulated among interested publishers, I remembered that she'd made a jump from television to publishing and sent her a message via Facebook to let her know about my project. Like me, she gets a thousand e-mails a day, but Facebook messages always stand out and she responded to my message right away, asking to see my proposal. Amid heated interest from several publishers, three days later, *Bulletproof Your Job* was sold to HarperCollins, in large part due to the strength of a long-term network relationship with this executive and in small part because of how a social networking site like Facebook can facilitate valuable real-time connections.

As the conversation winds down, resist the temptation to be a business card whore. Don't start papering the joint with your cards and stuffing your pockets with everyone else's. Offer to exchange business cards only with people you intend to follow up with or hope to connect with again on another occasion. And if when you get home you empty your pockets and find a card of someone you can't remember meeting, guess what? He didn't make much of an impression. But guess what else? If other people pull out your card and don't remember you, you didn't either. Get better at that.

Finally, it's lazy and dull of you to think that professional gatherings are the only places to network. A con man sees everyone he meets as a prospective mark. Sounds crude, but as a networker, you should, too. The FedEx guy, the person standing next to you in line at the airport, the man sitting next to you at the ball game, the woman in front of you in the bathroom line at the theater, everyone has the potential to offer a valuable connection to someone else. Keep your eyes and your mind wide open to the possibilities in everyone you meet. Lightning does strike.

▶▶▶ *Take everyday networking seriously.*
▶▶▶ *Build a network that will be a long-term resource to you.*
▶▶▶ *Weed, feed, and seed your network to keep it fresh.*

43. HELP THE PEOPLE IN YOUR NETWORK

The whole notion of networking can come off as kind of mercenary, suggesting the aggressive leveraging of another person's circle of friends or contacts for your own benefit. In truth, an effective network does give you access to other people's contacts, but you have to be prepared to give as good as you get. And even to give *before* you get.

Ineffective networkers approach the process in reverse, asking for favors even before they learn how to pronounce your name. They're the ones who sniff out how you may be of use to them and get right to the point of enlisting your aid.

Effective networkers don't want to discuss how you can help *them,* they want to know how they can assist *you.* They make it all about the other guy first.

When you focus on helping others in your network, your reputation and credibility grow. You make it clear you're not a taker, and your stature rises as those around you perceive you as a gatekeeper, someone with connections and insights you're more than willing to share.

Helping your network can range from making introductions to people within your company or your peer group to forwarding opportunities you discover to digging for information you think someone might need. A recent transplant to your area may need advice regarding which professional associations to join. A newly laid off coworker may need job leads or referrals. Your CEO's daughter may be on the hunt for a summer internship. Every time you become aware of a need, you've uncovered an opportunity to benefit someone by helping her make a connection. By doing that, you're also strengthening your ties on all sides as well as your network creds.

TRUE STORY

Some years ago, I met Don, a senior-level executive and father of four. To be honest, at first Don struck me as having somewhat of a superior attitude that wasn't terribly appealing. Shortly after I met him, the company he worked for was acquired and he was let go, leaving him jobless for more than a year. When he got back in touch with me, humbled by that long stretch of unemployment, I hooked him up with a former client whom I happened to know had a spot that was perfect for Don. I didn't earn a penny from making this connection (talk about pro bono), but Don became a goodwill ambassador and enthusiastic promoter of me and my company, pointing me to new business and eventually hiring me as a consultant. Don became another member of the sleeper cell of support for me in my industry. So did his new boss, by the way, who never forgot that he got a great senior executive for free.

Don't wait until someone asks for help. Look for ways to seed your network with leads and information and gossip that they might find useful. Forward articles or industry reports that might be of interest. Recommend vendors who've done an exceptional job for you. Pass along interesting job listings if someone's on the hunt. This makes it clear to your network friends that you constantly have them on your radar and that they can count on you in a pinch.

All of this is good old-fashioned workplace karma, and when it comes right down to it, you're only helping yourself.

▶▶▶ **Be an energetic and enthusiastic resource for the people in your network.**

44. BE ACTIVE IN PROFESSIONAL ASSOCIATIONS

Sometimes work can be so much work that the last thing you want to do is join a club or association that requires hanging out with people who want to talk only about work. Yes, professional association meetings have been known to be mind-numbingly boring from time to time. Even though the field of engineering is exciting to you, no one ever said the Amalgamated Engineers' monthly consortium would be some kind of frat party. But the fact is, time spent with your professional peers helps you keep your work and career in perspective. You meet people who face many of the same challenges you do, but who also many who enjoy the success you seek. And because you are involved with them outside of the context of your own job, it's a tremendous

TRUE STORY

Nick was an attorney specializing in intellectual property issues for a medium-sized firm. Though not exactly on the partner track, he had a solid niche and a secure job he was glad to have but not inspired by. At the annual convention of IP lawyers Nick rarely looked forward to attending, he hit it off with Dev, who was on the board of a tech start-up looking for funding. Nick stayed in touch with his new friend and six months later got a call from Dev inviting him to come on board as the new company's counsel. Nick jumped at the chance.

opportunity to interact with and learn from others in a positive environment that's free of office politics and other day-to-day pressures.

Participating in professional organizations is one of the best ways to bulletproof your job for the long term, because it allows you to keep up on industry gossip, hear who's hiring and firing, and share other information and ideas that can help you in your job and career. Such professional associations include organizations precisely related to your field (Google will help you find them if you don't already know what they are), as well as the Chamber of Commerce, the Rotary Club, Lions Clubs, unions, and other mixed-profession groups that share community-based interests.

Only an idiot chooses not to be involved in industry or professional associations. Usually this idiot talks himself out of it by fretting over the time he'd have to spend doing it, the price of membership, or the idea of all the networking he'd have to do at meetings and events. As I said, he's an idiot.

If you knew you could . . .

- ▶ Expand your network
- ▶ Learn about trends and emerging issues in your field
- ▶ Meet mentors or specialists who could help you broaden your knowledge or experience
- ▶ Strengthen your professional credentials
- ▶ Increase your professional profile
- ▶ Increase awareness of your company
- ▶ Find out what key players in your industry are doing
- ▶ Find out what other companies are up to
- ▶ Become aware of new job opportunities in your field

. . . wouldn't you do it *now*? Joining a professional association in your field is an investment of time and money that you will more than make back in valuable connections and innumerable resources you can tap in your work or when making a job change.

Once you join, don't just sit on your hands. Be an active participant. Attend meetings and conferences. Volunteer for committees or to work on the association newsletter. Make networking goals and meet them. Keep up the contact with people you meet.

▶▶▶ **Strengthen your credentials and your network by participating in professional organizations.**

45. PUBLISH ARTICLES AND DO PRESENTATIONS IN YOUR AREA OF EXPERTISE

Nothing screams "bulletproof" more than a place at the head of the room at a conference. Or your name featured prominently atop an article in a trade magazine or newspaper. The opportunity to present to industry peers or write articles for an audience of colleagues is an acknowledgement that you know your stuff. It's also an implied endorsement of your expertise that your employer can't ignore.

YOU DON'T HAVE TO WRITE IT YOURSELF

It's easy for me to say "Write an article" but I know how few people feel comfortable or confident putting their writing on display. Probably about as many as feel uncomfortable with public speaking. But if you have a great idea for piece, there's nothing stopping you from hiring a freelance writer at a Web site like www.asja.org or www.elance.com or partnering with a colleague who likes to write to create the article you have on your mind. You come up with the concept, provide the information for the article, and collaborate with the writer to nail down your vision for the piece.

N.B. Writers for hire are not collaborators, they're ghostwriters. If you don't want to share the writer's credit with your hired gun, negotiate that very clearly, in writing, in advance. There are plenty of writers who don't care about the credit when they're working for hire, but plenty of others do. And credit fights can get nasty, so work it out before a single word is written.

An equal colleague with whom you write your piece is a collaborator who will want to share the writer's credit—and the bulletproof benefit! Be aware that you are rarely paid for articles written for professional publications. So the reward for you and a collaborator is in receiving the professional credit of publication, while the reward for you and a writer for hire is professional credit for you and a fee that comes out of your wallet for the writer. If the publication is read widely by your superiors, that $50 an hour you paid the Harvard grad with an adroit pen could be worth it.

FINDING SPEAKING GIGS

Opportunities to present to an audience of your peers are all around you. From local, regional, and national professional organization meetings to annual conferences to gatherings of other trade groups, if there's a meeting, they need someone to speak. And there's usually more than one someone speaking, which means there will more than one opportunity for you to go after to speak.

Before inquiring about a speaking engagement, clear it with your boss. You don't want to step on her toes by going after a speaking gig she may want herself! If you get the okay to pursue it, you usually need to create a formal proposal. Outline a list of four or five topics you would feel comfortable discussing for twenty to thirty minutes that would suit the venue and boost your professional credibility. Then contact the organization's president to inquire about the possibilities. If you have a video of a previous gig that really sells you as a speaker, send it along with your query. And don't be shy about sharing positive feedback you may have received when you've spoken before.

Don't limit yourself to professional organizations either. Think civic organizations such as Rotary International, which has meetings fifty-two times a year, charitable groups such as Junior Achievement, local alumni groups, college courses, and trade associations that might be interested in your perspective, even if you're not from their industry. Every opportunity you snag to present or to publish adds to the credentials that will get you your next gig. And before long, you'll have a big fat CV loaded with published articles and presentations. Be sure to include all those career highlights in your resume and CV and bring all materials (including a portfolio of articles and DVD videos of your speaking gigs, if you have any) to every performance review to be sure your superiors know how you've been out there flexing your professional muscles.

It's not enough to just speak or write any old thing about what you do; you have to throw out a tasty bone, give them some dazzling tidbit to take away. This is how you become an authority on your topic—whether it's nanotechnology in banking or using YouTube in crisis management—by communicating with confidence and authority and mastery and skill. Just make sure it's related to your job. If it's not—if, for example, you're writing about making an orgasmic crème brûlée for a regional food rag when your day job is as an account supervisor—you're not bolstering your career, only showcasing what you do in your private life. Believe me, your employer doesn't care.

A TRUE STORY

Attorneys are required to earn continuing legal education credits (CLEs) by attending legal seminars in order to maintain membership in their state bar associations. Jon, a Delaware attorney, is frequently asked to speak at CLE seminars because of his background in criminal law, which few attorneys in his area have. Although the seminars take time to prepare, Jon knows this investment typically generates new clients for his firm. Following a session on practice pointers or defending a slip-and-fall case, he routinely gets calls from attendees interested in either referring business to him or asking for help on a personal matter. By virtue of his leading this seminar for his discerning peers, he is perceived to be the expert.

But let's not forget the personal PR for Jon, which his firm will happily exploit. It not only benefits from the clients recruited at said conferences, it's also able to brag on his attorney profile that Jon is a regular presenter at CLE seminars. His firm is able to share the spotlight and perceived expertise and cultivate new clients, and this, in turn, increases Jon's stature within the firm as well as his long-term bulleproofability.

Consider professional publications you read yourself as possible outlets. *The Wire Industry Standard* for folks in wire manufacturing, for example, or *What's Up Between the Covers* for people in book publishing. Even better, sneak a peek at the magazines or newsletters your boss, clients, and colleagues read. The audience for those rags is, of course, your ideal audience, because you're looking for a public airing of your expertise to raise your visibility within your industry and, more specifically, your company. If you're giving the keynote address at a conference on color trends in the auto industry and you work for DuPont, you're the Employee of the Week. Your efforts to shine a spotlight on what you know reflects positively on you *and* your employer won't soon be forgotten. Think your talk last month at that major trade show was overlooked? Not likely if your employers knew about it (see number 13, "Publicize your accomplishments").

But more important for your own professional prospects is the fact that the long-term boost you get from your exposure may well lead to unexpected career opportunities—particularly from the outside. The more people who get a load of your hot stuff, the more chances someone will think of you when an interesting opening occurs. You're creating your own luck here because you've salt-and-peppered your world with lively reminders of your expertise and overall appeal.

▶ ▶ ▶ *Hustle to get a byline and grab that speaking gig.*
▶ ▶ ▶ *Seek exposure that establishes you as an expert in your field.*

46. PAY ATTENTION TO WHAT YOUR PEERS ARE DOING

When you're clicking along happily in your own job, it's easy to ignore the zeitgeist among your peers. It's even easier to miss some of the big shifts that can happen in your field when you've got your nose in your work. Part of your ongoing job mainte- nance requires that you lift your head—regularly—and make a critical assessment of what's going on with your professional peers. Because whatever they're doing, you need to be doing that and more.

Start by taking the temperature of your immediate colleagues. What are the folks who have a similar job or are level with you in the hierarchy up to? Are they joining professional groups, attend- ing skills or leadership seminars, writing articles, and giving speeches—which I've already said *you* should be doing? If so and you had any hesitation or lacked motivation before now, you bet- ter kick into gear here and now. Are they coming in early, staying late, working weekends? Then you need to come in earlier, stay later, and work longer weekends. The tactics I've presented in earlier chapters of this book are meant to help you identify the norm, the bare average quality of work and behavior around you, and then to aim higher. This is more than keeping up with the Joneses in the competing cubicles all around you; it's about get- ting ahead and staying ahead of them so you can hang on to your job. If they're doing something bulletproof and you're not, you're at war with no armor, putting yourself at a distinct disadvantage when compared with your colleagues. So whatever they're do- ing? Do. It. Now.

Also, keep a close eye on what your professional peers outside your organization are doing. The best place to watch this is at

ASK YOURSELF:

▶ What am I reading to keep abreast of breaking news in my field?

▶ Am I ever able to share cutting-edge news or information with my peers?

▶ Who are the leaders in my field whom I look to as the gold standard?

▶ Who are the innovators in my field whom I look to for inspiration?

your association or trade group meetings and in trade publications. Listen to the chatter, find out what everyone's reading, and observe what's being discussed. Here's where you'll discover emerging issues, trends, hot topics, and gossip that your peers have gotten hold of before you did. Catch up quickly, and then make a point of getting a few steps ahead of them, particularly your doppelgängers at competing companies. You never want to be the last to know what's new.

▶▶▶ *Be alert to what everyone else is doing to get ahead.*

47. IMPROVE YOUR INTERVIEW SKILLS

Admit it: once you have a job, your interviewing skills go right to the attic for storage until "next time." Well, guess what? If you wait until "next time" to dust off your resume, your interview suit, and the savvy, steady, on-your-feet thinking that makes for a successful interview, it may already be too late.

Why should you stay interview sharp when you're happily ensconced in a job you love so much you might just keep it forever? Because you probably won't. And, like having money in the bank, being interview-ready is the kind of confidence you want to have.

Short of getting dressed up and interviewing yourself in the bathroom mirror, how can you practice and improve your interview skills? Start by revisiting the process, specifically the questions that commonly turn up in job interviews. Remember these?

- ▶ Where would you like to be five years from now?
- ▶ What achievement are you most proud of?
- ▶ Do you work best independently or as part of a team?
- ▶ Give me an example of a problem that you were able to solve with creative thinking.
- ▶ What would your last boss say is your greatest strength? How about your biggest weakness?
- ▶ What do you think makes you different from other candidates for this job?
- ▶ What excites you about what you do?
- ▶ How do you handle stress on the job?
- ▶ How would you handle a problem with a coworker?
- ▶ What's your favorite book?

You see why this is a good exercise: not only does it get your brain back into a strategic, sell-yourself response mode, it also gets you thinking about your current job in the context of the kinds of questions you may have been asked when you interviewed in the first place. Have you changed since then? Are your answers better now as a result of your experience in this job? Or are they worse? And when you ask yourself this question, which is often the concluding question in an interview:

▶ Do you have any questions about this job or the company?

. . . What do you wish you'd asked or known then that you know now? Heh-heh.

Ask yourself these sorts of interview questions periodically, say, as often as you update your resume and success documents. It's a handy way to be a weather vane of your own progress and satisfaction.

SO DO YOU WANT THE JOB?

Don't forget all those powerful nonverbal cues that you're eager, sincere, interested, and ready to hear their offer:

▶ Shake hands firmly and with confidence.

▶ Make eye contact, but don't stare.

▶ Sit up and lean slightly forward in your chair to indicate interest in what the interviewer is saying.

▶ Smile when appropriate to indicate you are friendly and easy to get along with.

▶ Keep your hands clasped in your lap; don't keep your arms crossed tightly on your chest; don't cross your legs, either.

▶ Nod to indicate agreement and that you've heard and understood the interviewer.

▶ Keep your hands away from your face and hair, as well as other parts of your body.

Use your performance reviews as an opportunity to think like an interviewee. People often think of their reviews as situations in which they need to defend themselves, respond to criticism, or make a case for a raise. Instead, treat every review like a job interview, where you're the picture of positivity and sell-sell-sell your accomplishments, qualifications, and abilities. Go into your review with your own agenda for promoting yourself. And of course bring your resume, success docs, and anything else that points up what a good job prospect you continue to be.

One more way to keep your interview muscles toned is to interview other people. Volunteer to participate in peer reviews or to be a part of a hiring committee or to interview prospective interns. Constantly touching base with your network of sleeper cells with this in mind is also good practice. Being on the other side of the interview desk helps you hone your own responses and to think like an interviewer.

Finally, even if *(especially* if) you're not looking for a job, if you're contacted by a headhunter or prospective employer, jump at the chance to be interviewed. It's the best way to keep your skills sharp and offers the perfect opportunity to see what's out there (see number 48, "Monitor the job market in your field").

▶ ▶ ▶   *Be interview ready at all times.*

48. MONITOR THE JOB MARKET IN YOUR FIELD

Whether the job market in your industry is hot or cold, keeping abreast of developments and trends will keep you ahead of the game and out of the line of fire. Being well informed about the job climate in your company, your company's competitors, and general shifts within your field will give you a priceless heads-up when bad news is on the horizon. Forewarned is forearmed, as the saying goes.

Do this by performing a SWOT analysis, looking at your industry's strengths, weaknesses, opportunities, and threats as if you were preparing a business plan for a new venture. Think like a CEO or business owner. What are your company's core strengths? What differentiates your business from your competition in a good way? What are the organization's weaknesses? Put another way, what are some roadblocks to growth or sales success? Given those strengths and weaknesses, what opportunities do you see now and in the future for your employer? What potential threats are looming on the horizon? Being able to answer these questions will help you spot career opportunities within your own company, as well as help you avoid departments that are due for hard times.

Other resources that are good to monitor include:

▶ Hiring reports. Watch which types of positions are being eliminated, which salary levels are being targeted, and which fields are experiencing worker shortages at Web sites such as TechCareers.com or HR.com, for example. Check which industries are hiring and which are about to go through yet another round of layoffs. Staying up on the job market will help ensure that your assessment of your market value and future prospects is on target.

▶ Job openings. A quick-and-easy way to spot trends is to routinely scan the job openings at major national job sites such Monster.com and CareerBuilder.com, as well as in your local newspaper. What types of positions are frequently listed, and

JUST SO YOU KNOW

Changing jobs or switching gears on your career is best done when the job market is up, not down. In other words, if the economy is dicey, work hard to bulletproof the job you have, so you can make a move at a more advantageous time. That said, if you're intent on making a job change during such times, target a competitor of the company you currently work for. That's where your best prospects will lie and your biggest value will be perceived. And if you just don't have the stomach to slog through a dreary job economy every time it happens, think about switching to a career in a field like nursing or education, which tend to be perennially safer. Finally, if your employer offers you "the package," to entice you leave when jobs are being cut, negotiate instead to keep your job at a lower salary, if necessary, so that when you decide to make a job move, you can do it at a time that's best for you.

which ones never are? Which fields are projected to grow in the next five years, and which will experience a decline? Are there any new terms and vocabulary being used in these job descriptions that you should pay attention to?

▶ Look outside your industry. While staying on top of your job, your field, and your industry is critical, sometimes looking beyond it, to other industries, can lead to some creative thinking. Don't limit your reading to just your own industry and trade publications; do a little sleuthing in related industries to see what's going on there. If you're in dental equipment and supplies, know all you can about that area, but don't stop there. Check into what's going on in dental hiring, dental marketing, dental surgeries, dental practice management, and medical equipment, for example. Know your industry as well as those that may impact or be impacted by it up and down the food chain.

A key benefit of being aware of the market is that you'll always be poised to go with the flow, including all the dips and curves that can affect your job and even point you to making adjustments in your career path. Having a broad and up-to-the-minute bird's-eye view will give an opportunity to send out your resume, make networking initiatives, and perhaps plan an exploration into a new industry poised for rapid growth—well before your cubemates ever knew what hit them.

▶▶▶ *Watch the job scene even when you're not looking for a job.*

▶▶▶ *Know how hard or easy it would be find a job if you were really looking.*

49. CONTINUE YOUR EDUCATION

You don't have to quit your job and go back to school to get additional education that will help bulletproof your behind. In fact, it's best to do it *while* you have a job, as going MIA from the workforce while you study will drop you from people's radar. Memories are short. If your intentions are to remain in your current field but broaden your knowledge base, do yourself a favor and hold on to the job while you seek enlightenment. Additionally, many companies offer to pay some or all of your continuing education costs; in which case, it would be sort of dumb to quit, wouldn't it?

Depending on your workload and the time commitment you

JUST SO YOU KNOW

Every time you read a book or an important article related to your work, find a way to mention it to your boss. He'll be impressed at your keeping up with your business reading on your own time, but he'll also benefit from what I call "borrowed reading." This is the information you share about what you've read that he can use as if he's read it himself. Yes, even your boss pretends to be reading the latest books and mags. What you tell him may prompt him to read it himself, but it may also let him off the hook from reading it at all.

I once had an assistant who was a voracious reader and who happily provided me with little summarylike reviews of everything she read, I think because she thought I was as avid a reader as she was. I wasn't. But her reviews were tremendously helpful in keeping me up on current books and other content, and it made me feel a little smarter, too!

have to make to your studies—which can range from a single three-hour seminar to three nights a week for several semesters—I guarantee it's totally worth juggling the responsibility. Here's why.

For starters, it will improve the skills you already have. When you get better at what you do, you increase your value because the people that matter will notice. Also, when you deepen your credentials, you are *perceived* as more qualified and valuable, meaning you markedly increase your earning potential. In education, an advanced degree can bump your salary up automatically, though this is rarely true in business. An MBA isn't quite the golden ticket it once was, but it is still pretty impressive to your boss and, these days, is a minimum requirement for certain jobs—even junior-level ones. But, once again, perception is everything, and potential employers *love* those advanced degrees, especially from snooty schools, because they suggest a pedigree that can improve the stature of the company by association.

Doctors, lawyers, teachers, and librarians *have* to continue their educations just to hang on to the jobs they have. You can do it, too—on your own time and maybe even on your company's dime—to make your pasture greener a little farther down the road.

Depending on your field and the new credential you seek, you may find yourself in class on a college campus, in a hotel ball-room, or parked in front of your computer taking in a lecture, completing coursework, or participating in a professional semi-nar. The Internet is by far your best resource for researching and identifying the best educational opportunities and most conve-

TRUE STORY

Rita was one of those people who had spent nearly a decade in various in-stitutions of higher learning, probably to avoid the plunge into the real world of work. Burdened by crushing college loan debt, she finally threw herself into a job search with a freshly granted Ph.D. in semiotics (what-ever that is) from a prestigious university under her arm. She was a good writer and had an idea that marketing was an area she should explore. She had no job experience to speak of, but luckily for her, she was interviewed by the CEO of a brand development agency who was awed by her fistful of expensive degrees. Rita ended up with a near-executive-level job for which she was wholly unqualified, an impressive title and an equally impressive salary, and a boss who insisted on calling her "doctor." Go figure.

nient venues for you. Distance learning is hotter than ever, with major universities offering degrees and courses specially designed to be completed online.

The point is that it's easier than ever before to find a way to pursue advanced degrees and other equally valuable certifications. And if you already have all the degrees and licenses and certs you want, do what every other successful person in business does to stay on top: read, read, read. Be an information sponge. Even if you are pressed for time or have a criminally short attention span, you can still invest your reading time wisely by subscribing to digests like those provided by SmartPros.com or services such as 800 CEO read.com that point you to what you *should* be reading.

The most important bulletproof point in this section: As good for you as all this education stuff is, it's only half as good for you as it ought to be if you aspire to stay with your company yet the company doesn't know about your pursuits. Every single course you take, every certification or credit you receive, every A you get on a paper is information you should share with your boss and HR. This should all go on your resume and be clearly pointed

UPSCALE DISTANCE LEARNING

You can join the ranks of high-end degree holders without ever leaving your desk. At Duke University's Fuqua School of Business, for example, you can earn an Executive MBA degree from wherever you are through its distance learning program. Connected to fellow students worldwide via the Internet, you watch lectures, complete group assignments, and turn in your homework. Check out distance learning programs at www.petersons .com/distancelearning.

out by you at your performance reviews, of course. Whether your company has helped you pay for it or not, it will feel that it has invested in your continuing education and will be less likely to fire you than the slob in the cube next to you who's been home watching reruns of *CSI: Miami* while you've been cracking the books and improving yourself.

▶▶▶ **Take advantage of tuition reimbursement offered by your company—if it's offered, your company thinks it's important.**

▶▶▶ **Extend your formal education now to increase your value in the future.**

▶▶▶ **Never stop educating yourself in informal ways.**

50. LEARN NEW SKILLS

I'm obsessed with learning a little more about what I already know how to do and with learning at least a little bit about doing things I don't know at all. It's partly curiosity but mostly bullet-proof instinct. There are all kinds of skills I've picked up over my career that were clearly outside my job requirements but have been incredibly helpful in forging relationships with people in other fields, allowing me to contribute to a variety of conversations, and giving me a general feeling of proficiency in various subjects (or at least enough proficiency enough to fake it!).

Look around you at work, and make a list of all the skills you don't have that would come in handy in your job. Say you're an editor. It would probably help to get your head out of the sand and acquire a basic knowledge of your company's design pro-

JUST SO YOU KNOW

I read an article in a Chicago newspaper some years back that both shocked and delighted me. It reported that in a poll of executives and HR professionals, the single most impressive thing on any resume was not an Ivy League degree or experience with a Fortune 100 company or even a Congressional Medal of Honor. It was that the job candidate had achieved the rank of Eagle Scout. Why do you think that is? Because Eagle Scouts are perceived to be dedicated, loyal, and, above all, in possession of a variety of superior skills the rest of us never bothered to acquire. You can't go back and become an Eagle Scout (especially if you're female!) but you can take some inspiration from just how impressive a fat sack of skills can be.

gram. And even if the in-house lawyers negotiate the contracts with your company's clients, wouldn't it be helpful if you knew how to read the contracts you're charged with fulfilling?

Some of these stretch skills you may learn formally through a class or seminar. Others you can pick up amateur-style, through basic research or even by just asking. Your corporate lawyer would likely be happy to give you a fifteen-minute tutorial on how to read a boilerplate contract. Your company's art director would probably be delighted, or at least encouraged, that you're interested in learning a bit of Quark and set you up with someone who can show you the ropes.

Take it upon yourself to develop your business writing or PowerPoint skills. Take a public speaking class. Learn a computer program that's brand new to you. Brush up on your high school French. Every new thing you learn or get better at improves your prospects for the long haul. How? More skills, more value. Or rather, the more skills *your boss thinks you have,* the more value. You'll also end up with a beefed-up resume and enhanced confidence in your own abilities that'll put a swagger in your step.

The columnist Carol Kleiman once said that there are eight terms that light up an employer's eyes and allow you to cut to the head of the line. They're languages, computer, experience, achievement, hardworking, overseas experience, flexible, and task-oriented. Half of those things are who you are, but the other half are things you can learn. So learn them! And then, as she said, move to the front of the line.

▶▶▶ *Never stop learning. Ever.*

BULLETPROOF TAKEAWAY

Being ready for any eventuality when it comes to your job is just common sense. It gives you the confidence you need to weather both the thunderstorms and the sunshine and blue skies at work. Your mother told you to wear nice underwear in case you're in an accident, right? This is the bulletproof-your-job corollary to that supremely good advice.

▶ Have financial resources socked away, a current resume at the ready, and a thriving network.

▶ Make yourself known to peers, decision makers, and opinion leaders in your field.

▶ Constantly improve and refresh your knowledge base by continuing your education and cultivating new skills.

Being ready is the hands-down best way to bulletproof yourself for the long haul.

ACKNOWLEDGMENTS

I wrote *Bulletproof Your Job* for friends, former colleagues, family members, and even viewers who have watched me on TV for years—all losing their jobs due to a struggling economy. These people have been victims of "rightsizing" and "downsizing," which are basically bullshit terms for being fired because a public company stock price went down a couple of cents or a small or midsized business owner believed all the media hype about a recession. Someone's got to pay, right?

As a headhunter and workplace expert, I knew there was something these tens of thousands of people getting laid off every month could have done to protect their jobs. That's why this book exists. But it would never have happened without an incredible group of people as committed to the value of my message as I am.

I have always been smart enough (and lucky enough) to surround myself with smart, loyal, hardworking, and dedicated people. My editor, Adam Korn, is tops among them. He grasped the concept and urgent value of this book from day one and moved triple time to speed this book to publication. He was thoughtful in his management of this project and really went the extra mile to make it happen quickly, for which I am deeply grateful. Thanks also to Stephanie Fraser, for her hard work and dedication to this book.

I feel lucky to be a part of the HarperCollins Business team, headed brilliantly by its publisher, Hollis Heimbouch. Hollis has incredible instincts and I'm grateful that she gets me, understands the pressing importance of this subject, and is fearless and determined in her drive to get this book swiftly into the hands of the people who need it most.

A very special note of thanks goes to HarperCollins Director of Creative Development, Lisa Sharkey, the first person to ever put me on TV as a workplace expert and among the first to see the real potential in this book. Her enthusiasm is contagious and she certainly enriched this publishing experience for me. I especially appreciate the friendship that Lisa and her husband, Paul Gleicher, a great residential architect, have shown to me over the years.

Steve Ross, Angie Lee, Doug Jones, Larry Hughes, Online Marketing Director Felicia Sullivan, and *all-time heroes* in the field of book production—Diane Aronson, Nikki Cutler, and Neil Otte.

I also want to thank Jamie Brickhouse of HarperCollins Speakers Bureau who keeps me booked on the road all year long (www.harpercollinsspeakers.com).

And, finally, thank you to HarperCollins President Michael Morrison, with whom I share the family and friendship of the wonderful Jeannie and Lou Bochette, who have generously provided their moral and emotional support to me for so many years. Talk about kismet!

Special thanks to Dave Hathaway of Barnes & Noble, a smart and dedicated executive who was generous with his sage and timely advice. Also special thanks also to my good friend Keith

Ferrazzi, author of *Never Eat Alone: and Other Secrets to Success, One Relationship at a Time.* Keith was an inspiration in writing this second book.

Now for the personal thanks. Brian Kuchta, who works for me and with me and has long been my conscience and my brain—*thank you.* I need Brian's valuable input on *everything.*

The most heartfelt thanks to Casey McNamara and my sister Laura Viscusi who have always been bulletproofing my job and my life and have both always supported me through thick and thin. Without the two of them, this book would not exist. Thanks also to Laura's husband Ross Garnick, a wonderful addition to my family and a great help to me. Warm thanks to my dear friend Russ Schriefer and his wife, author Nina Easton, who helped me with many ideas for this book. And thank you to Kyle Prandi for being such a supportive friend.

Some other special thanks—and they know why—go to Joseph Sullivan, Esq., Michelle and Jerry Birnbach, Jim Druckman, Chris Kennedy, and Mark Falanga; Rev. William J. Bergen, S.J., of the Church of St. Ignatius Loyola on Park Avenue in Manhattan; Elaine Peake, Dr. Gerald Pittman, Joseph Cohen, Carol Barnes, Michael Wolf, Vinnie Potestivo, Cameron Baird, Pam Tighe, Jessica Guff, Linda Stern of *Newsweek's Tip Sheet,* and Gennifer Birnbach. Thanks also to the folks at Ferrazzi Greenlight, including Love Streams and Ken Gillett.

Thanks also to Adele Scheele, Ph.D., author of *Launch Your Career in College;* Lars-Henrik Friis Molin, founder of Career TV and Careertv.com; Jeff Taylor, founder of Monster.com and an early supporter and first sponsor of my radio show, "On the Job;" Dick Boles, a dear friend and author of *What Color Is Your Parachute;* Harvey Mackay, an early supporter and author of *Swim with the Sharks Without Being Eaten Alive;* Shere Hite, Ph.D. a dear friend and an inspiration; Barbara Corcoran, founder of the Corcoran Group and author of *Use What You've Got and Nextville: Amazing Places to Live the Rest of Your Life;* and Tory Johnson, founder of Womenforhire.com and author of *Take This Book to Work.* Thanks to Eve Tahmincioglu of MSNBC.com; Neil Cavuto of *Fox Business News;* Stephanie AuWerter of SmartMoney; Lisa Belkin of *The New York Times;* Carol Kleinman, retired careers columnist at *The Chicago Tribune;* and Dalia Martinez, Enrique Rivera, and Neal Conan all of NPR's "Talk of the Nation." And, of course, thanks to Charles Gibson of ABC's "World News Tonight," who was the first to call me "America's workplace guru," on one of my many appearances on ABC's "Good Morning America."

Thanks to my late mom, Mildred Albanese Viscusi, who had one job her entire life—working at Macy's. She loved that job and taught me simple, hardworking values, especially about respecting my boss. She died of breast cancer at age 60 in 1993. My dad, a Parkinson's patient, also worked one job his whole life and retired after 40 years of being a newspaper pressman. These are the blue collar, hardworking people the whole working world used to be made of and I've been inspired by them all my life.

Finally, thank you to my literary agent and secret weapon, Karen Watts. I have known Karen since my first book, *On the Job: How to Make It in the Real World of Work,* but she really gave birth to *Bulletproof Your Job.* Karen worked tirelessly to make this book happen, while her husband and son ate cornflakes for dinner and had no wife or mother for two months. In part, my book is dedicated to her company, "Karen Watts / Books." Thank you, Karen.

Visit www.bulletproofyourjob.com to read my blog or to join the bulletproof conversation. You can also email me your bulletproof questions at stephen@viscusi.com.

Stephen Viscusi is a careers professional who has helped thousands of people succeed at work. A frequent contributor on the morning show circuit and NPR, he is the host of the nationally syndicated radio show *On the Job,* and he has been a featured careers and workplace expert in dozens of publications, including *The Wall Street Journal, The New York Times, The Washington Post, USA Today,* and *Fortune.* His company, the Viscusi Group, is rated one of the top ten executive search firms by *Crain's New York Business.* Stephen is also the author of *On the Job: How to Make It in the Real World of Work* (Three Rivers Press, 2001). He was born in Armonk, New York, and lives and works in New York City. He can be reached at stephen@viscusigroup.com and the book's Web site is www.bulletproofyourjob.com.